Between Fear and Hope

WERNER T. ANGRESS

BETWEEN FEAR & HOPE

Jewish Youth in the Third Reich

TRANSLATED BY

Werner T. Angress and Christine Granger

Columbia University Press   New York   1988

Published originally under the title *Generation zwischen Furcht und Hoffnung*
by Hans Christians Verlag, Hamburg.
Copyright © Hans Christians Verlag 1985
English translation and additional text copyright © Columbia University Press 1988

Library of Congress Cataloging-in-Publication Data

Angress, Werner T.
 [Generation zwischen Furcht und Hoffnung. English]
 Between fear & hope : Jewish youth in the Third Reich / Werner T.
Angress; translated by Werner T. Angress and Christine Granger.
  p. cm.
 Translation of: Generation zwischen Furcht und Hoffnung.
 Bibliography: p.
 Includes index.
 ISBN 0-231-06598-1
 1. Jüdisches Auswandererlehrgut Gross-Breesen. 2. Jews—Germany—
History—1933–1945. 3. Youth, Jewish—Germany—History—20th
century. 4. Farmers, Jewish—Germany—History—20th
century. 5. Jews—Germany—Migrations—History—20th
century. 6. Holocaust, Jewish (1939–1945)—Germany. 7. Germany—
Ethnic relations.
I. Title. II. Title: Between fear and hope.
DS135.G33J83213 1988
943'.004924—dc19
                                                    87–29797
                                                       CIP

Book design by Jennifer Dossin
Printed in the United States of America
Hardback editions of Columbia University Press books are Smyth-sewn
and are printed on permanent and durable acid-free paper

TO THE GROSS-BREESENERS
those alive and those who have died

Contents

Preface
to the American Edition

THE SUGGESTION to write on this topic came a few years ago from my friend and colleague, Professor (now emeritus) Dr. Werner Jochmann, then Director of the Forschungsstelle für die Geschichte des Nationalsozialismus in Hamburg, and his principal coworker, Frau Dr. Ursula Büttner. Although I was initially reluctant to embark upon an enterprise that touched my own past so closely, my friends in Hamburg ultimately persuaded me to proceed with it. Their arguments were threefold: I was a *Zeitzeuge*—a contemporary witness—having lived as a teenager through the period with which this study deals; I am a historian who, they trustingly assured me, would be able to approach the topic with objectivity and a sense of perspective, despite the fact that I was a "witness"; finally, after they saw the material on which such a study would be based, they said that it was unique in many ways and would be of considerable interest to potential readers. For having been a packrat all my life, long before I ever dreamed of becoming a historian, I had accumulated a fair amount of documentary material, some of which was made available to me by friends and acquaintances.

Once the original German version was decided upon, my friends in Hamburg advised me to address myself especially to today's young Germans, many of whom are not well versed in their country's recent past and who, upon reading the account, might even identify to some extent with my own generation half a century ago. I took this suggestion into account when I wrote the

ix

book, but at the same time tried to make sure that it would hold the attention of the older generation(s) of Germans as well.

The same holds true for the American translation. Somewhat enlarged in scope, checked through for errors, corrected, and in part rewritten, it aims at attracting readers from every age group in this country and the English-speaking world. There was an obvious readership, the children and grandchildren of German Jewish refugees who, I was told repeatedly after the German book appeared, are eager to learn about the origins and youth of their parents and grandparents but do not know German. But in addition, many people I know in this country, England, Australia, etc., often have rather strange misconceptions of what it was like to have lived, and especially to have grown up, as a Jew in Nazi Germany. Although most people today, here and elsewhere, know about Nazi terror—the Gestapo, the SS, the concentration camps, the "Final Solution"—few are aware that during the first six years of the Third Reich this terror apparatus, while very much in evidence behind the scenes, was not something that the regime emphasized. And as far as the German Jews were concerned, the six years before the "Crystal Night" pogrom on November 9, 1938 were a twilight period, a period when not fear of being killed (despite occasional violence against individual Jews throughout the country), nor even of being arrested (few Jews, for instance, were in German concentration camps before "Crystal Night") was paramount in their thoughts, but rather the constant humiliations, the growing isolation from their former non-Jewish friends, and above all, the slow economic strangulation that grew worse with every passing year.

But most people outside Germany, then and now, saw mainly the plight of their adult counterparts. Few knew or even gave thought to the lot of the young Jews, those who were teenagers or young adults when Hitler came to power in January 1933.

I hope that this book will remedy, at least to some extent, the general lack of knowledge on this aspect of the topic. At the same time, it is not a comprehensive history of German Jewish youth during the Nazi period; such a history remains to be written. But the book attempts to present in the first chapter a general picture of what it was like to live at a time when forces (to them

PREFACE TO AMERICAN EDITION xi

largely incomprehensible) turned Jewish schoolchildren into out-
casts, barred Jewish high school graduates from both employment and training, and made the search for a country to which
one might emigrate a slow, painful, difficult, and for a good
many, unsuccessful effort.

The second chapter, supported by the documents that follow
it as chapter 3, is a case study of an emigration training center
where a group of young Jews went to learn farming and other
occupational skills which, they hoped, would ultimately facilitate their emigration from Germany. The group at Gross-Breesen
in Silesia was both representative and not representative of German Jewish youth in general. It was representative inasmuch as
before their arrival at the training center the boys and girls had
undergone most of the same humiliations, the same sense of isolation in school, and for some in their jobs, as had most of their
peers throughout Germany. And, like them, they also faced the
search for a country that would accept them. Furthermore, in
November 1938 boys and young men 18 years old or older shared
with 30,000 male Jews the ordeal of being imprisoned in a Nazi
concentration camp, following the pogrom known as "Crystal
Night."

Conversely, their experience was not representative because
Gross-Breesen was the only large emigration training center for
non-Zionists. Most such centers that sprang up at that time—
and the first chapter discusses this development at some length—
prepared young and sometimes not-so-young people for emigration to Palestine. While before 1933 only a very small segment
of German Jews subscribed to Zionism, after Hitler took over a
growing number of Jewish parents sent their children to Zionist
"Hachsharah" ("Preparation") camps, since at first Palestine offered the best opportunities for prospective young immigrants.
The group in Gross-Breesen did not want to go to Palestine but
to some other country overseas. Many of the young trainees came
from the German-Jewish youth movement, which gave a special,
somewhat elitist stamp to the entire community. But although
Gross-Breesen was a rather special place, as the documents in
particular will show, working and learning experiences there were
similar to those of the Zionist Hachsharah centers.

In short, what this case study hopes to accomplish is to per-
sonalize an experience undergone by a substantial number of young
German Jews in the 1930s—an experience not widely known.
It tries to show, in part through the voices of individual people
at the time, what it was like to grow up in Nazi Germany as a
Jew. Although the first part of the book makes it clear that until
the November pogrom a *relatively* "normal" life was still possible even for young Jews despite the steadily deteriorating situation, the documents concentrate on what we now know was
the beginning of the end of a traditional Jewish existence in Germany, and beyond that, the first step toward what came to be
known as the "Final Solution of the Jewish Question," affecting
most European Jews beyond Germany's borders as well.

In closing, I want to express my sincere appreciation to those
who have helped me in the preparation of the American edition
and who made it possible to submit the completed manuscript to
the press by the deadline agreed upon. I am very grateful to
Barbara Beresford and Sara Duke for typing portions of the
manuscript, and to Christine Granger who shared with me the
job of translation. To the staff of Columbia University Press,
and especially to my editors, Kate Wittenberg and Karen Mitchell,
go my warmest thanks for their support and encouragement during the preliminary stages of translation and revision, and for the
care and attention they gave to the manuscript while getting it
ready for publication. Donna Albertus graciously volunteered her
help for the index. Finally, it is understood that all errors and
other shortcomings which this study may contain are exclusively
my responsibility.

Acknowledgments
to the German Edition

I WANT TO express here my thanks to all those who helped me to complete this study. Grants from the Fritz-Thyssen-Stiftung and the Historische Kommission zu Berlin provided financial support and enabled me to spend the summer of 1981 and the first six months of 1984 doing research in Berlin and Hamburg. In Berlin I was a guest of the Historische Kommission and its successive chairmen, Professor Dr. Otto Büsch and Dr. Wolfgang Treue, along with the members of their staff—Professor Dr. Stefi Jersch-Wenzel, Dr. Jürgen Schmädecke, Ms. Marga Siebeck, Ms. Monika Koch, and Ms. Sigrid Kleinschmidt. I want to thank them warmly for their advice and assistance.

I am equally indebted to the Director of the Forschungsstelle für die Geschichte des Nationalsozialismus in Hamburg, Professor Dr. Werner Jochmann, and to his staff, Dr. Ursula Büttner, Dr. Werner Johe, Ms. Irene Roch, Ms. Lieselotte Trappe, Ms. Adeline Verino and Ms. Angelika Voss-Louis. All of them gave unfailing assistance during the various stages of research and in preparing the manuscript for the printer. But my very special thanks go to Dr. Werner Jochmann and Dr. Ursula Büttner, who initially suggested that I write on the topic. Then, throughout the time it took to complete the work, they gave me valuable advice, encouragement, and criticism, and, going far beyond the usual editorial procedure, supervised every single step of the publication process.

While working in archives other than those of the Historische

xiv ACKNOWLEDGMENTS TO GERMAN EDITION

Kommission and the Forschungsstelle, I was helped by their staffs, notably the ladies and gentlemen of the Geheimes Staatsarchiv Preussischer Kulturbesitz, Berlin-Dahlem, and of the Leo Baeck Institute, New York. To all of them go my thanks, though in particular to Dr. Sybil Milton, who helped me greatly with her competent advice.

I also owe a debt of gratitude to the following persons who provided me with relevant material, references, and information, both written and verbal: Dr. Ernst G. Lowenthal, Berlin; Mr. Thomas Jersch, Berlin; Dr. Harvey P. Newton, San Jose, Costa Rica; and Mr. Ernst Cramer, Berlin. Last but not least, I want to express my warmest thanks to Ms. Uta Drews, Berlin, who made many stylistic corrections in the introductory chapter of the manuscript and at the same time gave its content a thorough and critical reading.

Needless to say, any mistakes, false interpretations, or other flaws that may remain are solely my own responsibility.

Between Fear and Hope

1. On the Situation of Jewish Youth Under Hitler

ON JANUARY 30, 1933, the aged German Reich President, Paul von Hindenburg, instructed the leader of the National Socialist German Workers Party (Nazi Party), Adolf Hitler, to form a government. This act of Hindenburg's that day was to have fateful consequences for the Jews in Germany, and subsequently for those beyond its borders as well. But at the time the significance of this event was recognized by only a very few, for of course even the most pessimistic Jews (and non-Jews) were unable to fathom the dimensions of the catastrophe that ultimately was to befall them. Those most immediately affected by the National Socialist "seizure of power" and the anti-Jewish measures that very soon followed were the Jewish children and young adults. The older generation, established predominantly in business and the professions, at first was affected only in part by the "legislation on Jews" (*Judengesetzgebung*) that began on April 7, 1933 with the Civil Service Act, by which "non-Aryan" officials (a newly coined term) were ousted from their posts.[1] Those engaged in business and trade, however—and they constituted the vast majority of German Jews—were generally able for some years to continue earning a living.[2] Conversely, education and vocational or professional training for Jewish youth were restricted on all levels nearly at once, partly as a result of the official measures, partly because of mounting anti-Semitism in the public schools, workshops, and firms that was systematically encouraged by government and party officials. Thus, the prospects of young Jews for a normal life in Germany were negated step by step nearly from the outset of Nazi rule.

This development, however, was neither uniform nor abrupt. As is well known by now, the entire National Socialist Jewish policy remained erratic, selective, and arbitrary until the end of 1938, and in part even beyond this point.[3] This was due on the one hand to the rivalry between state and party, especially the various government departments, party offices, etc., and on the other to the consideration the Nazi leadership gave during the first six years of the Third Reich to the economy and especially foreign trade, neither of which was to be jeopardized by a too-rapid exclusion of Jews from Germany's business world. Finally, neither the leading echelons of the state bureaucracy nor those of the party had a clear or, above all, unified conception on how to proceed specifically with the "Solution of the Jewish Question." Agreement existed on only one point: to get rid of the Jews as soon as possible by gradually mounting pressure that would force them into emigration. The result of this reasoning— it can hardly be called a "policy"—was a gradual increase of anti-Jewish legislation and decrees that curtailed the civil rights of Jewish citizens bit by bit, restricted their occupational spheres, and triggered periodic anti-Jewish demonstrations, in part begun and organized by local party organizations, that quite often led to acts of violence against Jewish individuals or their business establishments. But since legislation and street riots had no visible connection; since individual acts of violence (*Einzelaktionen*) were in fact officially prohibited[4] and, except for Boycott Day of April 1, 1933, occurred sporadically and locally until the pogrom of November 9, 1938 ("Crystal Night"), many Jews clung for years to the illusion that their situation perhaps might not be quite hopeless, would at least not get worse, and thus would allow the older generation to remain in Germany and endure. Jewish youth, of course, could not stay on but eventually would have to leave the country. However, even the latter realization did not predominate among German Jewry until the passage of the racial laws at Nuremberg in September 1935, and a good many clung to their hopes until after Crystal Night.

To be sure, it was all an illusion. But during the initial years of the Third Reich, only a very few Jews saw this. When Jewish and non-Jewish commentators today frequently condemn these people for their blindness and reproach them directly or indirectly for not having foreseen the gas chambers of Auschwitz and Treblinka, one can only deduce that such critics have wrong notions about the situation then prevailing.

What was it like? Aside from the fact that most German Jews were deeply rooted in and attached to their fatherland, which had shaped their cultural tradition, their education, language, thoughts, and emotions to such an extent that any thought of having to leave it was incredibly painful to them, immigration into other countries was far from easy in the nineteen thirties. The world was in the throes of one of the worst economic depressions in modern history, with massive unemployment everywhere. Under these conditions which country would welcome an influx of refugees who might conceivably become public burdens? In addition, there were strong anti-Semitic currents in most countries, in Europe as well as overseas, and this was another obstacle to mass emigration. Ultimately the Jews had only two choices: to resign themselves to Hitler's regime and the changed conditions that came with it, to adapt, present a low profile, and retrench; or to endure the traumatic break with everything familiar and dear to them and to overcome the fear of an unknown, alien country where they would have to build a new life from scratch under difficult circumstances.

The gradual elimination of Jews from the life of the nation— "creeping persecution," as one historian has called it—[5]was particularly injurious to the young generation of Jews, who in many ways were even more severely affected by National Socialist policies than were their parents and grandparents. Young people too, experienced the impact of the anti-Jewish measures in varying ways.

First, much depended on where a young Jew resided. In big cities such as Berlin, Hamburg, Cologne, Breslau, Frankfurt am Main, or Munich, the prevailing anonymity provided a good deal of protection, at least during the first six years of the Nazi regime. Equally important were the support and comfort that the large Jewish communities in the cities would give to their members. Furthermore, substantial segments of the population in the urban centers, especially the working classes in cities like Berlin, Hamburg, and Cologne, for instance, were not fanatical supporters of the National Socialists and their racist philosophy even when they conformed outwardly, and Jews were aware of these sentiments. Needless to say, here, too, were variations. Thus, in Nuremberg, where the publisher of the pornographic and Jew-baiting scandal sheet *Der Stürmer,* Julius Streicher, was also governor (*Gauleiter*) of Franconia, neither urban anonymity nor the considerable size of the local Jewish community could offer protection against the outrages committed—with blessings from on high—by anti-Semitic thugs, notably during the annual party rallies.[6]

But on the whole, life in the big cities after January 1933 was easier for most Jews living there than for those in small towns and villages. For in the countryside, there was no anonymity; Jews were well known by everybody and were easy targets for anti-Semitic acts of aggression. And in contrast to the prevailing situation in the cities, the relatively small, scattered Jewish communities in the rural regions could not offer their members much support, especially since rural anti-Semitism, which had been endemic in many parts of Germany long before Hitler came to power, was now officially sanctioned. No wonder, then, that from 1933 on increasing numbers of Jews migrated from the rural areas to the big cities, particularly Berlin, or, whenever possible, left Germany.[7]

Aside from one's area of residence there were other factors that led to variations in the ways in which individual Jews, including the young generation, were affected by the policies of the regime. Children from assimilated families—until 1933 the vast majority of German Jewry—faced their Jewishness differently from those who came from a Zionist or pronouncedly religious background, at least until the passage of the Nuremberg Racial Laws in September 1935. Zionist idealism, but also adherence to the traditionalism of religious practice, gave strong support during those troubled times to those who were committed to either. In this respect, children from assimilated homes had a much harder time of it, as in many instances their parents'

religious bonds as well as their own were merely formal or entirely absent. Like their parents, such youngsters saw themselves
first and foremost as loyal Germans, and their religious affiliation with Judaism was to them primarily a "private matter" of
secondary importance. Now the National Socialists robbed them
systematically of their German identity. Yet, in spite of the steadily
worsening conditions, children from assimilated homes found it
much more difficult to accept the necessity of emigration than
did their Zionist or religiously Orthodox peers, especially, as
was often the case, if their parents kept on hoping for years that
Hitler's state would not last long. For this reason, their parents
neither made efforts to emigrate nor encouraged the children to
do so.[8]

In addition to differing attitudes Jews held toward Zionism,
the religious heritage, and one's German identity, it was equally
significant whether one came from an affluent and usually also
intellectually and culturally receptive home, or from an impe-
cunious one. Young people fortunate enough to come from well-
to-do backgrounds and whose parents decided to emigrate nearly
always found it easier to leave the country than did children whose
families were poor. Well-to-do fathers were generally business-
men, lawyers, or physicians who were successful in their respective vocations and who applied their capabilities and often
connections abroad to work purposefully for their emigration, or
at least for that of their children. The longer the National Socialist regime lasted and the stronger anti-Semitism became, the
truer it was that affluent Jews eventually opted for emigration
when those financially less well endowed did not. The tendency
of the latter was usually to retreat, cowed as they were, into the
privacy of their homes and there to wait and see what turn developments would take.[9] For the most part lacking either personal or business connections abroad to facilitate their emigration, they also had not enough money to purchase the treasured
immigration visa—during the early thirties not infrequently
available for a "fee," especially at certain South American consulates—or steamship tickets. Conversely, for all those, regardless of background, who had joined a Zionist youth movement,
had gone "on Hachsharah" (agricultural training) and subse-

quently "on Aliyah" (emigration to Palestine), the financial circumstances of the parents did not matter. Especially Jewish immigrants from eastern Europe (*Ostjuden*)—who generally lived
under exceedingly poor conditions in the worst slums of the big
cities, and who since 1933 had been hardest hit by the brown
terror—left for Palestine as soon as they possibly could with the
aid of the Zionists. And in contrast to their more affluent and
assimilated coreligionists, they did not have much to abandon as
they left, neither worldly goods nor memories of a once-beloved
homeland, as Germany had never been a real homeland to the
majority of them.

It was likewise significant whether a young Jewish boy or girl
continued school after the age of 14, when attending school was
no longer obligatory, or became an apprentice in order to learn
a trade. In the latter case, much depended on whether the training was in agriculture or a skilled craft, on the one hand, or on
the other whether that person was to learn a business. Business
training did not offer good chances for emigration during the
thirties, since all countries, except for the Soviet Union, suffered
from the severe effects of the Great Depression and for the most
part had more people trained for business than they needed. In
the end, the question of whether to continue with one's school
education or train for a trade was frequently settled in favor of
school, and in most cases the decision was determined by the
parents' social and economic position. That a high school diploma (*Abitur*) offered fewer chances for emigration abroad than
did a certificate of apprenticeship in a skilled trade was more
often than not ignored.

Finally, the factor of how a Jew of any age looked to non-
Jews determined to a large degree his or her freedom of movement in public, at the workplace, or in school. Life was more
difficult for anyone who "looked Jewish" or who had a Jewish-
sounding name. "Jewish looks," though, remained a rather elu-
sive concept to many non-Jews—and not only for those who
lived in parts of the country where they had never even met a
Jew face to face—as they had completely wrong notions on the
matter. Their image of what a Jew allegedly looked like was
determined, consciously or unconsciously, by the anti-Semitic

caricatures in Nazi smearsheets such as *Der Stürmer*, among others, thereby creating a stereotype to which the majority of German Jews did not conform. This goes far to explain why young people such as Joel König, Inge Deutschkron, Valentin Senger, and others were able to pass as "Aryans" and, with the help of false papers, survived Hitler's genocide.[10] But even those whose identity was fully known to their fellow students or coworkers usually had an easier time avoiding harassment or worse if they did not look Jewish. The same held true for names: whoever was called Lewinsohn or Cohn was thereby "branded" as a Jew.

As we now turn to problems that Jewish youth as a whole had to face because of the Nazis' "Jewish Policy," it should be understood that this brief summary cannot do more than provide an overview for today's generation. The term "Jewish youth" as used here means above all, although not exclusively, those boys and girls who were born between 1915 and 1925 and thus were old enough in 1933 to have experienced consciously the events and consequences of the National Socialist "seizure of power." Here are the figures: according to the national census of mid-1933 there were 499,682 Jews living in Germany. This number included only those who affirmed their identification as Jews; it did not include those who had been baptized or who were "racially" considered "non-Aryan" because one parent or perhaps even only one grandparent had been Jewish. The above figure declined by 1937 approximately to 350,000 and by the end of 1938 to 297,000.[11] In 1933, the Reichsvertretung der deutschen Juden (roughly, "National Representative Agency of German Jews")[12] estimated the number of Jewish children who were of compulsory school age—thus those born between 1919 and 1927—as roughly 60,000.[13] Since obligatory school attendance ended at 14, the above figure does not include Jewish youngsters who had gone on to high school (*Gymnasium* for boys, *Lyzeum* for girls). Nor does it include all those who had graduated from elementary school (*Volksschule*) in 1933 and had become apprentices in either business firms or craft establishments. In 1937, an administrator of the Reichsausschuss der Jüdischen Jugendverbände (National Committee of All Jewish Youth Organizations) estimated that the number of Jewish youths 10 to 30 years old who were still in Germany at the beginning of that year was 85,000.[14] Since half of the young Jews born between 1915 and 1920 emigrated in 1933, 1934, and 1935, as has been established at least for the State of Württemberg, and approximately another 25 percent of this group in 1936 and 1937, we may assume that the better part of the 85,000 youths belonged to the younger age groups, encompassing those born in 1921 and after.[15]

Under ordinary circumstances, young people growing up in the majority of industrialized nations since the mid-nineteenth century could count on receiving a regular education in school and, thereafter, vocational or professional training. This had also been the educational pattern that children of Jewish citizens in Germany had followed for nearly a century. With Hitler's appointment as Reich Chancellor and the subsequent path to National Socialist dictatorship, this right, uncontested for generations, was now questioned for Jewish children. As early as February 12, 1933, the Reich Commissioner for the Prussian Ministry of Science and Education, Bernhard Rust, had stated in an election speech that "he would cut away with every bit of brutality dictated by duty whatever was un-German [and] did not belong in German schools."[16] A little over two months later, on April 25, 1933, the "Law Against Overcrowding of German Schools and Universities" was passed, and the First Implemental Order accompanying it specified that henceforth the enrollment of Jewish children in schools and universities could not exceed 1.5 percent of the total student body in any educational institution. In the case of those already enrolled, the total percentage of Jews was to be reduced to at most 5 percent. Only children of war veterans who had fought at the front lines, and of foreigners, were exempted from this *numerus clausus*.[17]

This still comparatively "mild" law constituted the beginning of a process by which the young Jewish generation was systematically excluded from all educational state institutions. As a result, those who survived the Third Reich were frequently deprived of a solid education. For although Jewish schools were founded in response to the exclusion, most of them could not replace, either qualitatively or quantitatively, the state-run secondary schools, except for a very few Jewish schools in some of the bigger cities. However, the expulsion process was first and foremost the result of psychological pressure, for until the decree of the Reich Minister for Science, Learning, and Popular Education was passed on November 15, 1938, ordering all Jewish children still attending state schools to leave them, no prior laws regulating Jews' attendance of secondary schools and universities were passed on the *national* level.

Nevertheless, those who were able to remain in state schools before November 1938 did not enjoy the same rights allotted to their non-Jewish peers. Discrimination against them ranged widely: they were no longer eligible for reduced tuition, were prohibited from visiting public swimming pools or school hostels in the countryside (*Schullandheime*), and a directive was issued to the effect that there would no longer be an entry under the heading *Charakter* (i.e., behavior and personality) on their report cards. These are but a few examples of how young Jews from 1933 on were subjected to mounting discrimination in the public schools. The harassments were intended to show them that they were different from their peers, "racial inferiors," and this, of course, contributed to making them feel humiliated and isolated.

To be sure, Jewish pupils at the time had differing experiences, some of which were less painful than others. Thus in schools located in big cities they tended to be less exposed to persecutions by teachers and fellow pupils than were those who attended schools in small towns or villages—though even in the urban centers there were vast differences from one school to the next. But on the whole, the pronouncement of the Reichsvertretung, in a report issued in 1934 that "Jewish children and adolescents who are attending non-Jewish institutions of learning are suffering damage to their personality development"[18] was undeniably correct. Like so much of what was then published by Jewish organizations for informational purposes, this statement was couched in very euphemistic terms. After all, one could not very well use the word "persecution" in such a report, though it was well known that Jewish children were being treated increasingly as pariahs by teachers and fellow pupils. Positive school experiences were the exceptions that proved the rule.[19]

Let us look at a few recollections of that period. One witness

born in 1926, writes about his school days from 1933 to 1937 in
the town of Lippehne in the Mark Brandenburg: ". . . Between 1933 and 1935 my sister completely lost her Christian
friends . . ."; as for him, "nobody wanted to sit next to me,
nobody wanted to play with me during recess." Although the
homeroom teacher spoke up for him rather courageously in front
of his classmates, nothing changed because the non-Jewish children did not dare to be seen with Jews or, worse, to befriend
them, even if they might wish to. He goes on: "For us children
the years from 1935 to 1937 were actually better than the first
years of the Nazi regime had been, only conditions in school
deteriorated from year to year. We had come to accept that we
were non-Aryan and prohibited from playing with any Aryan
child. For this reason we stayed among ourselves."[20]

Another, unnamed witness who grew up in a small town near
Aachen describes how he became an outcast in school, a black
sheep with whom nobody wanted to play, except for the only
other Jewish boy in his class. A similar experience has been
related by a woman born in 1921 who grew up in Wittlich, close
to the Luxembourg border. She attended a Catholic school of the
Ursuline Order and was the only Jewish child in her class. Before Hitler came to power she had liked school. But the good
relations she had had with her classmates changed in 1933. Nobody wanted to talk with her; whenever she tried to make contact
anyway, she was pushed away. And another girl from Worms,
also born in 1921, fared no better. Her teacher, a woman, did
not miss an opportunity to make anti-Semitic remarks in front
of the class or to harass the Jewish girls. The girl's best friend
stopped associating with her between one day and the next, and
even stopped greeting her.[21]

Valentin Senger, born in 1918 and camouflaged as an "Aryan,"
had to endure the hate tirades that his music teacher unleashed
against Jews: "There I sat in silence and had to listen to the
crimes allegedly committed by my people—all delivered in the
music teacher's oily voice. . . . How I cursed my silence, the
constant sufferance, that failure to protest! My entire subsequent
life has been marked by these experiences. Even now I apologize
twenty times a day for everything and nothing. . . . My bash-

fulness, insecurity, inconspicuousness that were forced upon me
so that the family might survive account for these constant apol-
ogies of mine."[22]

Similar accounts have come from many locations: Danzig,
Nuremberg, Frankfurt/Main, even Neu-Schwienowitz. One need
not be a psychological expert to empathize with the difficulties
young German Jews faced at the time in growing up. They lived
in a hostile environment, attended school in that environment,
and there were exposed to derision, abuse, and at times beatings
merely because they were "different" from their "Aryan" classmates. And far from trying to put a stop to such discrimination,
the authorities actually supported these acts in the name of National Socialist racial doctrine.

It might be useful to supplement the reports of former victims
with two recollections by non-Jews who, during the Nazi period,
had Jewish classmates. One, Rudolf Augstein, publisher of the
West German magazine *Der Spiegel,* writes that until 1936 there
was one Jewish boy who, as Augstein puts it, was the "black
sheep" of the class and as such subject to persecution by his
young peers. As this was a school for the humanities (*huma-
nistisches Gymnasium*) and not science, "Simon" (not his real
name, according to Augstein) was never actually beaten; but he
had to suffer insults and humiliations, and had to be at the service of his classmates.[23] A second witness, Jürgen Gäde, now a
school principal in Kassel, who received his secondary education
in Berlin during the thirties, recalls an incident involving his former biology teacher, Dr. Gerd W., who taught "racial theory"
(*Rassenkunde*) in his class. One day Dr. W., dressed in Nazi
uniform and decked out with the party insignia and the emblem
of the National Socialist Teachers League, was supervising the
students during recess in the school's courtyard. When a piece
of paper slipped out of a running youngster's pocket, the teacher
ordered a physically handicapped Jewish student to pick up the
paper. But before that student could move, a non-Jewish boy
from a lower class rushed over and bent down to pick up the
offending piece of paper. Dr. W. thereupon "took a hasty step
forward, stepped on the paper whereby his knee collided so
strongly with the head of the onrushing boy that the latter dropped

to the ground." Simultaneously, Dr. W. yelled: "If I order R.
[the Jewish student] to pick up the paper, then the Jew will pick
it up!"[24] Needless to say, there were other non-Jews who at the
time noticed the effects of racial discrimination on their Jewish
fellow students; they were then in no position to do anything
about it, but they did remember.

To alleviate this psychological and emotional pressure, and at
the same time wanting to create for those young Jews who had
already left the state educational institutions schooling facilities
as close in quality to the state schools as possible, the Reichsvertretung made a tremendous effort to create more Jewish schools.
This was no easy task. In 1933, of the approximately 60,000
Jewish children still subject to compulsory education, roughly
15,000 attended 80 existing Jewish schools. Of these, approximately 10,000 were in elementary schools, and the other 5,000
went to ten secondary schools of which only five were authorized to issue a certificate of graduation that qualified those students who had passed the final examinations (*Abitur*) to proceed
for study at a university. The remaining five were intermediate
secondary schools (*Real-* or *Mittelschulen*). Of the 70-odd Jewish elementary schools that were operating in 1933, only about
20 to 25 had curricula of a quality comparable to those of the
state schools. The most urgent tasks then faced by the Reichsvertretung were to increase the number of Jewish schools on both
levels; to expand those already in existence; to adjust the curricula to the changed situation as of 1933 and, above all, to en-
rich them. This required a great deal of money. In 1933, the
Central Committee of German Jews for Aid and Development
(Zentralausschuss der deutschen Juden für Hilfe und Aufbau), a
section of the Reichsvertretung, made 103,537 Reichsmarks
available for this purpose. The various individual Jewish communities and parents, respectively, had to raise each an additional third of the total costs. During the years that followed, the
number of children in Jewish schools as well as the number of
the schools themselves increased. In December 1937, there were
23,670 children going to 167 Jewish schools. At the same time,
the number of young Jews still subject to compulsory education
had dropped to about 39,000. This meant that over 60 percent

of Jewish children subject to compulsory education now went to Jewish schools, whereas in 1933 it had been only 25 percent, that is, 15,000 of around 60,000.[25]

Given the circumstances, the difficulties of keeping such a school system going mounted from year to year. It became increasingly harder to find qualified teachers, who had been in abundant supply at first after they were dismissed from state schools until many of them emigrated. Moreover, the number of local communities and parents able to finance Jewish schools had also declined by the end of 1938, likewise owing to emigration but also to internal migration from villages and small towns into large urban centers. Furthermore, the incomes of Jews shrank, and growing numbers of them became unemployed. These factors increased the financial burdens of the Central Committee for Aid and Development, especially since it also found itself in each consecutive year with fewer funds. In spite of all these obstacles the Reichsvertretung succeeded until nearly the onset of the final catastrophe in maintaining a (constantly diminishing) number of Jewish schools. Exact figures, however, are no longer available for the period after November 1938.[26]

For most Jewish children the transfer to these new schools was a veritable deliverance. "Suddenly I found myself in a different world that I could not at first fully grasp—too beautiful to be real" wrote one person, who at the age of 12 in 1938 had entered the Joseph Lehmann School in Berlin.[27] Joel König, who in 1937 at the age of 15 was enrolled, likewise in Berlin, in the *Gymnasium* "Adass-Isroel" of the Jewish community, and who was at first somewhat overwhelmed by the demands that were made on him there, realized also with relief the contrast to his former school: "How insignificant were the difficulties [I] encountered with foreign languages in comparison to the positive changes which this Jewish institution of learning brought into my life. Gone was the evil nightmare of Jew hatred. There was no longer a picture of the Führer; there were no more *Sieg Heils*, no unfair brawls, and no Nazi fighting songs. Liberated, I was allowed to breathe freely."[28] Even Inge Deutschkron, who had experienced no unpleasant incidents when she had gone to her Berlin *Lyzeum* and who was by no means enthusiastic when her parents made

her transfer to the vastly overcrowded Jewish *Mittelschule* in the
Grosse Hamburger Strasse, nevertheless acknowledged that "the
attempts of this school—but also of other Jewish schools—to
carry out their tasks as best they could was a considerable
achievement, . . . given the prevailing special circumstances."
But the real oasis for her was the Jewish sports field in Berlin's
Grunewald: "Everything oppressive that weighed heavily upon
us even in school was there no longer evident."[29]

The Jewish schools did not merely dispense knowledge. Beyond this primary task, they also tried to strengthen the pride
and raise the Jewish self-awareness of their young charges. The
signal to do so had been given by Martin Buber as early as August 1933. In an article entitled "How Do We Educate an Open
(*unbefangen*), Independent New Generation?" Buber wrote:

I have suggested—so far without success—founding . . .
an educational office (*Bildungsamt*) for Germany's Jews. By
this I do not mean an emergency barrack but a solid edifice,
even if it is due to an emergency that we are forced to build
it. And I do not visualize the Jewish school [system] which,
I hope, we shall create, to be a mere asylum for children no
longer able to remain in the general public schools where they
cannot prosper anymore, but a genuine home, planted on solid
ground, true to our character and destined to prevail.[30]

Buber's call did not go unheeded. Already in its first report,
in December 1933, the Central Committee for Aid and Development went on record to say that "we can state in general that
the Jewish schools are attempting to make the overall instructions more [consciously] Jewish in nature in order to convey to
the growing youths the degree of emotional support that they will
require for their future life and the struggle for their livelihood."
In order to coordinate the means by which Jewish values were
to be conveyed as uniformly as possible, in January 1934 the
Educational Committee of the Reichsvertretung issued "Guidelines for the Draft of Lesson Plans for Jewish Elementary Schools,"
with a supplementary commentary by then secondary school
teacher Adolf Leschnitzer.[31]

The guidelines reflected the inner conflict that their authors

were facing at the beginning of the second year of Hitler's dictatorship in regard to the future of the Jews, and especially the
young generation. To some extent they still seem to have har-
bored hopes that young Jewish people might remain in Germany
after all. For how else can we explain that in the first paragraph
of the guidelines, under the heading "General Goals," there is
mention of the "twofold prime experience [Urerlebnis], inherent
within every Jewish child alive, a Jewish and a German one"?
This supposition obtains additional credibility through the subsequent comment "that everything which Jewish existence and
Jewish thought owe to the German spirit [Geist] and, conversely,
all that which Jewish spirit and Jewish creativity [Arbeit] have
contributed to the development of German culture, is to be revealed [during classes] in its interrelationships." To be sure, this
passage was inserted as a supplement to the official state guidelines pertaining to the teaching of German, which were binding
for Jewish schools as well, and may therefore have been inter-
polated for tactical reasons. But regardless how one interprets
these two passages in particular, the authors of the guidelines
(for the *Jewish* schools) still seem to have clung to their belief
that a German-Jewish symbiosis continued to exist, however
modified in form, and under rather aggravating circumstances.
Furthermore, the fact that the word "emigration" was not mentioned anywhere in the guidelines is another indication that such
an attitude may have prevailed. For although a reference to the
"buildup of Palestine" was made specifically in connection with
the teachers' task of creating a vital understanding "for the eternal values of Jewish religion and Jewish life in the present time,"
no further elaboration followed. Mention was also made, in connection with the "necessary vocational changes" (*Berufsum-
schichtung*), of the need for learning one European language and
modern Hebrew, and in geography classes "information on Palestine . . . is to receive special attention." But it sounded all
rather vague, if not embarrassed. Only Leschnitzer referred at
one place in his commentary openly to Palestine as "the most
important destination for Jewish emigration."

   There is no doubt, though, that the Jewish element was to be
strongly emphasized during instruction. Jewish spirit was to per-

meate the school. Every child was to "acquire a healthy awareness of . . . [his or her] Jewishness; . . . [he or she] was to
learn gladly what this meant, with every bit of pride and sacrifice
this entailed." For this reason, "things Jewish" were to be made
"the core of all subjects suited for them," thus, notably in religion, Hebrew, biblical and Jewish history. Willpower and a
sound character were likewise vital educational objectives, together with physical exercise, i.e., gymnastics and sport, as well
as manual training. As to the latter, Leschnitzer commented: "We
want to educate people who do not look at the trend toward the
acquisition of manual skills—something that has so far remained
outside the purview of significant numbers of Jews—merely as
a necessary evil, but who grow up with the feeling that such a
way, too, can lead toward a harmonious way of life." Here, in
Leschnitzer's commentary, the necessity for occupational retraining emerges much more strongly than in the guidelines, though
it is not entirely clear whether the acquisition of manual skills
was seen primarily for a future abroad, especially in Palestine,
or also in Germany. All uncertainties that still existed in regard
to this point in 1934 were eliminated a year and a half later, on
September 15, 1935, when the "Reich Citizen Law" and the "Law
for the Protection of the [German] Race" were announced at Nuremberg. From then on there were no doubts left to any reasonable person that Jewish youths, at least and above all, would
have to emigrate and, on account of the innumerable difficulties
connected with such a move, would have to be appropriately
prepared and trained. A few months later, in 1936, a Jewish social worker wrote that "the Jews now face the task of having to
emigrate from Germany on the largest possible scale," regardless
of whether economic necessity dictated such a step. Therefore,
the "earliest possible transplantation of the young generation must
receive priority. For youth still possesses the ability to readjust
and to sink roots into new soil, [qualities] essential for success."[32]

This view began to gain widespread acceptance within German Jewry. Indications that the young in particular were facing
hardships accumulated rapidly. Every year 5,000 to 6,000
youngsters were leaving school, and it became increasingly dif-

ficult to secure for them opportunities for vocational training. The comment of a Jewish observer at the time put it in a nutshell: "Our youths are not unemployed; they are devoid of an occupation."[33] Added to this were the restrictions that governed the enrollment of Jewish students in universities. Many who had originally planned to study for an academic career now found themselves barred from doing so. As a result, a growing demoralization took hold of an entire generation of young German Jews who, after September 15, 1935, were no longer even full citizens but merely second-class citizens with very restricted rights. "I was an adult when I was thirteen," a woman born in 1925 recalled, "—not only I—but every other child in similar circumstances. We had no choice."[34] And another witness, writing about his childhood, states that at the age of 13 he read newspapers attentively and worried about the situation of Germany's Jews.[35]

Although especially the occupational prospects of Jewish youths in Germany were steadily deteriorating from year to year, it would be wrong to think of them as having lived, ever since January 1933, in constant fear, perpetually unhappy and viewing the world around them solely through the windows of their parental homes, virtual prisoners. For until November 1938, most of them were able to move about fairly freely, travel, visit the theater or movie houses, dine in restaurants, and engage in similar activities. Many of them availed themselves of the various opportunities. To be sure, there were also limits. Some restrictions arising from the differing individual, social, and economic circumstances among German Jewry have already been mentioned; in the cultural sphere, too, the range for unhampered movement was narrower in the provinces and especially the rural regions than it was in the larger cities. Moreover, even in the cities a gradually increasing number of restaurants, public swimming pools, theaters, movie houses, and the like had signs reading either "Jews not wanted here" or "Forbidden to Jews," which effectively blocked their use of such facilities. To some extent at least, an alternative for those barred from "German" places of entertainment was provided by the officially sanctioned creation, in 1933, of the Kulturbund deutscher Juden (Cultural Association of German Jews, subsequently called

Jewish Cultural Association), which over the years attracted a
steadily increasing clientele.[36]

Yet even more important for the morale of the young generation than cultural events was the Jewish youth movement. Its
influence remained strong until the last of its various groups were
banned following the November pogrom of 1938. As greater depth
on the subject would be beyond the scope of this book, only a
few of its most important aspects can be touched upon. Like the
non-Jewish "German" youth movement out of which the Jewish
one evolved and after which it was modeled, the Jewish movement—Zionist and "assimilated" non-Zionist—was likewise
composed of numerous small and larger groups and *Bünde*
(roughly, associations or leagues).[37] The first of its kind, "Blau-
Weiss, Bund für Jüdisches Jugendwandern in Deutschland" (Blue-
White, *Bund* for Young Jewish Hikers in Germany) had been
founded before the First World War. Form and content such as
hiking trips, uniforms, camp fires, evenings at a group's den
(*Heimabende*), and the songs were all acquired from the German
youth movement. After a while the Zionist organizations adopted
Jewish ideas, traditions, and songs, largely under the influence
of Martin Buber.[38]

From 1933 on, the Zionist youth movement, like Zionism as
such, began rapidly gaining new followers. For until January
1933, Zionism and the youth groups associated with it had remained a numerically rather small minority within German
Jewry, although its members made up for their small numbers
by being articulate and intellectually very much alive. With the
onset of the Third Reich, Zionism received a tremendous boost.
For as a movement it offered, to youth above all, a concrete
prospect for emigration to Palestine. And when the last non-Zionist youth organization was ordered dissolved in 1936 by the
Gestapo, the Zionists had the field all to themselves. This was
not accidental.

Within months of the National Socialist "seizure of power"
all Jewish youth organizations in Germany, 97 in total, had to
register with the Office of the Reich Youth Leader (Reichsju-
gendführung). Then on November 2, 1933, this Reich Youth Office appointed the National Board of Jewish Youth Organizations

(Reichsausschuss jüdischer Jugendverbände), which had been founded in 1924, as "the solely responsible central organization of Jewish youth," authorized in this capacity to discuss with the Reich Youth Office all matters pertaining to Jewish youth groups.[39] Tight supervision, however, was not exerted by the Reich Youth Office but rested with the local police, notably the political secret police, the Gestapo. As early as summer and fall of 1934, the range of activities open to Jewish youth groups was being increasingly curtailed throughout various parts of Germany. They were forbidden to wear uniforms, to appear anywhere in public in formation, to hike or camp in groups. The Gestapo justified these prohibitions in one of its monthly situation reports, published in the fall of 1934, by claiming that the Jewish youth movement "constituted a deliberate provocation vis-à-vis the German public" because "these children were still behaving in a cheeky and impertinent manner." The same Gestapo post, in Potsdam, had complained a few weeks earlier about the "large gatherings of Jewish youth" in public, and then had accused the Reich Youth Office of apparently condoning the mass appearance of "Jewish boy scouts at German lake shores" where, "because of their noisy and impudent behavior, they were rapidly becoming a general nuisance."[40]

It soon became apparent, though, that the Gestapo measured the various Jewish youth groups by vastly different yardsticks. Those who were Zionist received preferential treatment because they were actively advocating emigration. Thus, the Gestapo post in Frankfurt on the Oder reported on August 30, 1935 that the Zionist youth organizations had recently increased their membership considerably; for this reason "the activities would be supported in every way in the interest of a growth in the emigration figures."[41] Conversely, those youth groups and associations who continued to advocate that Jews should remain in Germany, i.e., the assimilationist organizations, encountered constantly mounting repressive measures from the police. Thus, one of the two largest Germany-oriented Jewish *Bünde*, the Schwarzes Fähnlein, Jungenschaft (Black Troop, Boys' Force), was put under so much pressure by the authorities that in December 1934 its leadership decided to disband. Two years later the Ring, Bund deutsch-jüdischer Jugend (Ring, League of German Jewish Youth), which at that time had already been compelled to change its name to Bund der jüdischen Jugend (League of Jewish Youth), suffered the same fate.[42]

What was the special attraction of the Zionist and non-Zionist youth movements during the Third Reich? For the children of the educated and well-to-do Jewish middle class, the youth movement had already had a strong appeal during the Weimar Republic. It then grew rapidly after 1933, notably the Zionist segment. In 1932, all Jewish youth leagues together encompassed approximately 26,000 members, thus about 25 to 30 percent of all Jewish youths in Germany. In 1936, there were 50,000, thus roughly 60 percent of the total number.[43] Such growth was the logical result of the increasing isolation of especially those boys and girls who did not go to a Jewish school immediately after the Nazis came to power in 1933. As children and adolescents, they generally suffered more under the discriminatory practices they encountered than did their elders. The latter were able in many instances to maintain their relations with non-Jewish friends and acquaintances of long standing or, if these relations started to disintegrate, to deal with the reasons for such a development rationally. Conversely, many youngsters, notably those at the age of puberty, reacted purely emotionally and more violently than their parents did. And as they were now shunned by their former peers as pariahs, they became receptive to new circles of friends and thus often joined a Jewish youth group.

A further consequence of the new situation after January 1933 was the discovery of things Jewish and of Jewish values. To be sure, very few of these young people turned overnight into devout Jews, especially if they had not been brought up in their homes in the traditional Jewish ways. This, too, happened, but usually more by way of exception than as a rule. But the fact that they suffered discrimination simply because they were Jewish awakened their self-consciousness and forced them to accept the affiliation with this religious community and its history dating back over two thousand years, a community that had been persecuted again and again without being extinguished despite persecutions, and that had contributed decisively to give the world many of its ethical precepts and moral challenges. Primarily the Zionist youth groups did their part to impart Jewish traditions and knowledge, frequently all but forgotten or never even known by the boys and girls, and to bring these to life. This was often done without necessarily emphasizing religion as such. The objective was to strengthen first and foremost their awareness as Jews and their pride in being part of a larger Jewish community. Such consciousness, coupled with the relief of being with peers their age and exposed to the same hardships, lent to many of these young people an inner strength that their parents by then were no longer able to give to them. In this way, every year a growing number of boys and girls found in the Jewish youth movement a spiritual and psychological home and, at the same time, a marked Jewish identity.

Another important function of the *Bünde* was to help young people prepare for emigration. The leading representatives of Germany's Jews, especially the Reichsvertretung, allotted this task top priority after the passage of the Nuremberg Laws. And when they decided that as many young people as possible were to be given an opportunity to receive occupational training in either agriculture, a handicraft, or both, they were given full support by the youth movements, both non-Zionist and Zionist.[44]

The ideal of the "simple life" (the title of one of Ernst Wiechert's novels, a book familiar to most Jewish and non-Jewish youngsters organized in *Bünde* during the thirties) was deeply rooted in the tradition of the German youth movement, regardless of the particular orientation of each of its numerous groups. Since the youth movement was founded at the end of the last century, its members had emphasized their close ties to nature, the German landscape, the peasantry (*Bauerntum*). Here was certainly a forerunner of what in the Nazi period came to be known as "blood and soil romanticism." An attachment to and understanding of nature, a sense of communal solidarity, and the resolve to become upright, high principled, life-affirming, and all-around capable people—such were the principles and objectives that even before the First World War a rebellious youth had held up against the prevailing Babbittry of their elders, most particularly the urban bourgeoisie. These ideals had become intrin-

sic to the Jewish youth movement as well, regardless of how
individual organizations differed in their thinking in other areas.
Among the Zionist groups these views were reinforced by the
ideologically motivated, practical task of preparing young Jewish pioneers for the building of settlements and a productive farm
life in Palestine, although the Zionist movement had formulated
these objectives long before 1933.[45]

A few non-Zionist training facilities for future farmers, gardeners, and craft workers created to restructure the occupational
patterns of Germany's Jews had existed for some time before the
Nazi period. Most of them were intended to accommodate young
and, above all, poor Jews. As early as 1893, the Israelite Educational Institute at Ahlem near Hanover, subsequently known
as the Jewish School of Horticulture at Ahlem, was founded; it
existed until the summer of 1942. In 1928, under the sponsorship
of the Jewish War Veterans League (Reichsbund jüdischer Frontsoldaten), the landed estate Gross-Gaglow near Cottbus was put
into operation for a similar purpose after purchase by two Jewish
agencies, the Reichsbund für jüdische Siedlung (Reich League
for Jewish Settlement) and Jüdische Landarbeit GmbH (Jewish
Farm Work, Inc.). In addition, from 1922 there was the Neuendorf estate near Fürstenwalde, not far from Brandenburg. It served
as a training facility for unemployed Jews.[46] Thus, when the need
for systematic planning of emigration led the Jews, in 1933, to
tackle the problems of providing suitable occupational training
for youths simultaneously with the occupational retraining of
adults, several appropriate training sites were already at their disposal. At first, however, progress was very slow, because the
Jews were not at all clear as to what to expect or how to react
to the momentous political changes ushered in with Hitler's appointment as chancellor. In the first annual report of the Central
Committee of German Jews for Aid and Development only the
"*Possibility* of Jewish settlement activity" was mentioned, leaving open the question of whether such activity should take place
inside Germany or abroad. The authors of the report also pointed
to the need for putting the Gross-Gaglow estate, which was in
financial straits, back on a sound footing and concluded their
report with a statement that in retrospect looks rather peculiar:

"Agrarian-political legislation of the German Reich during the past year [1933] has clearly shown that *in the foreseeable future German Jews will have no feasible opportunity for agricultural work on small farms . . . of their own.*"[47] But as the next two years were to show, there would be not only no opportunity for Jews to work on their own holdings, but there were increasingly fewer agricultural and handicraft training facilities available to Jewish apprentices or training assistants (*Praktikanten*) on non-Jewish farms and in non-Jewish workshops. At the end of 1935 the Reichsvertretung talked about the continued "shrinking of training facilities accessible to Jews in non-Jewish enterprises" and added that there were even difficulties in Jewish firms because the trade guilds (*Innungen*) and trade associations refused to accept Jewish apprentices. In anticipation of the additional 6,000 Jewish children who would leave school in April 1936 and would increase the number of those in search of occupational training, the Reichsvertretung now gave serious consideration to the "accommodation of the greater part of Jewish youths in communal Jewish training facilities."[48]

It was not easy at first to obtain official sanction for the creation of such training facilities. As early as 1933 there were difficulties regarding the Gross-Gaglow estate because officials in the Prussian Ministry of the Interior worried that the 29 Jewish settlers there, whom they would have liked to get rid of, might instead attract other ones. This caused quite a stir among the bureaucrats concerned. In November 1933 the district administrator (*Landrat*) of Cottbus in charge of the matter wrote to the Ministry of the Interior that although the gardening work at Gross-Gaglow was "unobjectionable . . . , the remaining tasks, in particular those connected with the purely agricultural settlement, were done very poorly because of the well-known aversion Jews had toward physical labor." In his view it would be "imperative in the interest of quiet, order, and security to remove the Jewish settlers," as the "Aryan" inhabitants of Gross-Gaglow felt threatened by them, especially since they—the Jewish settlers—were all newly married and one could anticipate a considerable increase because of births. As it turned out, these worries were needless. On July 5, 1935 the Gestapo post at Frankfurt/

Oder reported—by way of proving that the Zionist idea was making great strides among Jewish youth—that most of the Gross-Gaglow settlers had departed for Palestine.[49]

Gross-Gaglow was only one of the first examples of the difficulties that Jewish youth faced in finding suitable agricultural training facilities inside Germany. During the second half of 1934 the matter was being scrutinized by the Gestapo as to what basic policy should be adopted, apparently at the suggestion of the then Prussian Minister–President, Hermann Göring. On September 14 Reinhard Heydrich—then still only head of the Gestapo—reported to Göring that in June of that year he had told the Reich Minister of the Interior, in regard to the training and retraining of Jews in agriculture and handicrafts, that the Gestapo had no objection to the creation of "closed [training] camps" where Jews would be turned into farmers and craft workers as long as these facilities made emigration, specifically to Palestine, easier. But under no circumstances were Jews to be encouraged "to create for themselves a field of activity, either in agriculture or in handicrafts, in Germany proper." And at the end of his report Heydrich pointed out that "as of and including April 1934" 2,158 Jews, presumably for the most part young people, were already being retrained; because of this "flooding of agricultural regions with Jews . . . . , justified indignation" had been aroused among the populace. For this reason Heydrich requested that a basic policy on this problem be developed as soon as possible.[50] To comply with his request, a meeting was called on November 27, 1934, in the Reich Labor Ministry, with a representative of the Gestapo being present. Nothing is known about the exact nature of this meeting. What did emerge from it was the decision—apparently arrived at after painful deliberations—to allow the creation of Jewish emigration training centers, although various Gestapo officials kept a jaundiced view of the matter. Thus, the reporting officer of the Gestapo post at Potsdam wrote in July 1935 that the people of the Teltow district were up in arms about the Youth Federation of State Zionists (Jugendverband der Staatszionisten) at the Neuendorf training center because "the Jews there were becoming increasingly cocky and impertinent."[51] As will subsequently be shown, the founding of the only non-Zionist training center, Gross-Breesen, initially also faced opposition from local administrators and party officials. All in all, it took quite a while before the bureaucrats expressed themselves officially on the question of whether or not to permit young Jews to become farmers or handicraft workers at special training centers. Formal basic approval came only in the spring of 1936. The provisions issued to this effect by the Reichsnährstand (Reich Food Supply Agency)[52] stipulated that, "as a matter of principle, Jewish-owned farms were to be placed [first] at the disposal of Jews for their agricultural training." Only after all such available possibilities had been exhausted could farms of non-Jewish owners be used as well. This ruling was a success for the Reichsvertretung.[53]

Meanwhile, actual preparations for training that would facilitate the emigration of a steadily mounting number of young Jews had progressed both in Germany and in neighboring countries. By the end of 1935, the Reichsvertretung reported that over 2,587 boys and girls were involved in such training.[54] Whereas placements of individual trainees with non-Jewish farmers or artisans decreased in number from year to year, new training centers geared to provide education in agriculture, handicrafts, or housework began to spring up from 1935 on. With few exceptions—such as some very small enterprises near Berlin, Hamburg, and Frankfurt/Main as well as the Jewish Agricultural Training Center Gross-Breesen, which was founded in Silesia in 1936—they were run by the Zionists and served to prepare young people for settlement in Palestine. At the end of 1936 there were 30 training facilities of varying size and capacity, and in 1937 5 more agricultural estates began operation. On September 30, 1938, 5,520 Jewish youngsters were working in a total of 94 training establishments. However, by the end of that year only 61 were left, 20 of them rather substantial agricultural and gardening farms with a total of 1,190 young trainees. Thirty-three smaller facilities had fallen victim to the November 1938 pogrom. Shortly thereafter, most of the remaining ones were either forced to close down or at least lost their status as training centers.[55]

The task of equipping and, above all, supervising all these different training centers fell to the Reichsvertretung. Its board

of directors, which consisted overwhelmingly of prominent assimilated German Jews even after it was reorganized in April
1935, was working closely with the Zionists in all matters pertaining to training and emigration. Until 1933, relations between
Zionists and non-Zionists—who constituted the great majority
of German Jewry up to that time—had been rather strained. This
changed under the impact of National Socialist racial policies.
At the latest after the implementation of the Nuremberg Laws of
September 1935, cooperation grew noticeably closer between the
Reichsvertretung on the one hand, and the Zionist movement,
including the Palestine Office (Palästina-Amt) and Hechaluz, on
the other.

The Palestine Office, located in Berlin, might be described as
Zionist headquarters in Germany. Its principal task was to issue
the coveted immigration certificates for Palestine, the number of
which was fixed by the British government of the mandated ter-
ritory. Hechaluz was a Zionist organization that had been founded
in eastern Europe in 1917 and that was politically neutral. In
1921 it had extended its activities from its central location in
Warsaw to the entire world. Its German branch (*Landesver-
band*), established in 1923, had approximately 8,000 members.
Its main function was to prepare young Jewish people for a life
as workers and settlers in Palestine and to help them with their
emigration to that country. Although originally it had not been
a youth organization as such, after 1933 it increasingly adopted
many of the traits of one. Together with its parallel organization
for orthodox Jews, Brith Chaluzim Datiim—or Bachad, as it
was usually referred to—and in closest connection with the Palestine Office, Hechaluz organized Hachsharah (training) and
Aliyah (immigration into Palestine) for those young Zionists eager to leave Germany. Thus, Hechaluz and Bachad together formed
a kind of umbrella organization for the Zionist youth groups in
Germany, but also paid attention to young individuals not organized in federations or *Bünde* who were interested in possibly
settling in Palestine. In this way, boys and girls who had never
been in a *Bund* met up with members of youth groups in the
various training centers.

Because of the special political conditions prevailing in 1933, the Zionist *Bünde*—Habonim, Hashomer Hazair, Werkleute, Makkabi Hazair, to name but the best known—had created a two-track training and emigration system: Youth Aliyah and Middle Hachsharah (*Mittleren Hachscharah*). To a certain extent the Youth Aliyah was the more privileged of the two, inasmuch as it strove for the fastest possible departure of boys and girls between 15 and 17 years of age to Palestine where they would receive their occupational training. The selection of those who could join Youth Aliyah was made primarily by the *Bünde*, and although nonorganized young people also joined Aliyah, those organized in youth groups—who in 1936 constituted 75 percent of the young people in Zionist training centers—had a distinct advantage. Thus, it is not surprising that the great majority of young Jews who went to Palestine with Youth Aliyah came from organized Zionist youth groups. Until March 1938 they amounted to 2,184 boys and girls, and one year later to a total of 4,635.[56]

Middle Hachsharah was planned for those who for some reason could not participate in Youth Aliyah. They were for the most part children who had left school, usually between 14 and 16, who were going to training centers in either Germany or neighboring countries. Here, too, the youth movement dominated, for the leaders assigned to the various training centers by either Hechaluz or Bachad came nearly exclusively from the Zionist *Bünde*. The number of youngsters who were trained in this fashion in 1937 amounted to approximately 800.[57]

There were several reasons why the number was not larger. First, many parents still refused to consign their children to a future of "social decline"—for as such did they view training for an agricultural or handicraft occupation. As late as the beginning of 1938 Georg Josephthal, a man who had dedicated himself energetically to furthering such training, complained that during the past five years it had not been possible "to convince the German Jews that manual occupations did not constitute a degradation vis-à-vis those in either business or the academic world." Second, as the same observer had pointed out a year before, 70 percent of the girls did not receive a solid occupational education. "Parents keep their children at home to help with the housework or use them in other ways as cheap labor and thereby deprive them of suitable occupational training." A third reason was that approximately 30 to 40 percent of all Jewish youngsters in Germany were either physically or psychologically unfit for any communal training course.[58] From this it follows that those young people in the Zionist-run Hachsharah centers and, as will be shown later on, those who went to the only non-Zionist emigration training center, Gross-Breesen, constituted a kind of elite, a "youth aristocracy."

Hachsharah centers existed not only in Germany but also in France, Luxembourg, Holland, Belgium, Denmark, Sweden, Lithuania, Poland, Czechoslovakia, Yugoslavia, Italy, and the British Isles.[59] These facilities were open to young German Jews, too. Unfortunately, though, after the conclusion of the ordinarily two-year training course, they were not permitted to stay abroad but had to return to Germany unless they had the (rare) opportunity to move on immediately to either Palestine or some country overseas. With that, Hachsharah training abroad had only limited value.

What was it like in practice, the occupational training of the Hachsharah centers in Germany and abroad? The Reichsvertretung and those special agencies associated with it bore the financial burdens and determined the economic and legal aspects, while Hechaluz and/or Bachad supervised the actual training. Those Zionist youth groups that predominated in the various Hachsharah centers were thus in a position to determine life within them—pedagogically, culturally, and socially.[60] This was of considerable importance inasmuch as the boys and girls who "went Hachsharah" more often than not lacked a solid school education, but had to be prepared nevertheless to acquire language skills and to adjust psychologically to the future immigration into Palestine. In addition, they had to become adjusted to communal agricultural work and community life in general, something which amounted to a new experience even for those who belonged to a youth group, as most of them came from middle-class urban families and had been raised for the most part as individualists. To cope with these problems, the instructors—*Madrichim* in Hebrew—were carefully selected, and the lesson plans and educational schedules thoroughly worked out. In principle there was an attempt to restrict the physical work of those newly trained to six hours a day so that there would be at least two hours left for intellectual work. The subjects to be taught were strongly and consciously tied to the Zionist world view: Hebrew, area studies of Palestine, history of Zionism, Judaic studies formed the core of the curriculum. But in addition there were classes on agriculture and handicrafts and, for the girls, household skills as well, for instance, in sewing, cooking, canning, baking bread, etc. Whenever possible, the trainees also received instructions in natural sciences, mathematics, German orthography, and grammar, to name but a few. Although the curricula differed in some specifics from one training center to another, the basic overall program was adhered to by all of them.[61]

One common aspect that, in retrospect, emerges very clearly from various reports written during the thirties is a genuine sense of dedication, of idealism, that permeated most of the training centers, both Zionist and non-Zionist. "There is someone working doggedly trying to build an Aliyah chest," wrote one *chaluz* (pioneer) from the Hachsharah camp at Niederschönhausen near Berlin in 1936. "His body moves two and fro with the plane. He is all concentration, and beyond the task at hand there are the dreams. Aliyah! That's what most of us dream of. That's our goal, that's what we are working for. Blue-white! In the field glows the star [of David]!" And another wrote from the same place: "Our goal: to become a worker, a little cog within the large gear that is Palestine!"[62] One observer from a different, unnamed Hachsharah facility dwelled on the "Jewish experience": "Over and over again, spontaneously intoned by somebody, our old songs are heard, telling us about the creation of a new Jewish people rooted in the spirit of its forefathers. Everything Jewish, regardless of which motives and in which regions it first developed, we are trying to convey to our trainees [*Menschen*]."[63] Very similar views were voiced by one of the training assistants (*Praktikanten*) at Gross-Breesen, the only major training center for non-Zionists. "For us, the decisive question is whether we'll succeed in turning the people here into true Jews. General education and human understanding alone cannot do this. . . . The objective that we have in mind is the creation

of a communal settlement of Jewish people [somewhere overseas, but not in Palestine]. . . . Our settlement must become a
contribution . . . to the revival of Jewish life. Therefore Jewish
education here in Gross-Breesen cannot be a matter of secondary
importance. . . ."[64]

Yet despite the generally successful attempt to turn young people, who for the most part had grown up in cities, into farmers
or gardeners, and despite the intensive efforts to win them for
Zionism, it was not always easy to arouse the enthusiasm of
everybody on Hachsharah for the projected worker's life on a
kibbutz in Erez Israel, i.e., Palestine. One who survived the Third
Reich inside Germany later depicted the difficulties he encountered during his—admittedly rather brief—stay at the Hachsharah training camp at Schniebinchen early in 1940: "I was very
unhappy there. All others were older than I was, nor was I physically and mentally as far developed as could have been expected
of a boy 13 years of age. . . . Life there had a military tinge,
and I was neither used to nor prepared for it. On certain days
one was expected to change one's underwear. . . . Of course,
one had to make one's bed and also change sheets all by oneself.
During the three months I was there I never did change sheets,
nor did I ever give my underwear to be washed."[65] Another one,
who was being trained at Jessen as well as in Neuendorf, found
the job of harvesting beets particularly "the worst agricultural
labor" he ever encountered.[66]

Joel König, too, had many reservations about his experiences
on "Kibbutz-Hachsharah" at Steckelsdorf, where he was trained
from December 1939 until May 1942 under conditions much more
difficult than before the war. He did not take kindly to the "ugly
Zionist jargon" that prevailed there as a "language all its own,"
and by way of example cited the following: "It occasionally happened that the youth leader announced at supper: Chawerim, I
have been informed by Merkas that they have organized in Berlin an advanced Ivrith course for Madrichim. (Comrades, I have
been told by the central office that they have organized in Berlin
an advanced Hebrew course for youth leaders)." Equally strange
to him were the "songs and dances of Erez Israel that belonged
to the Zionist rites." After a few months of cramped communal

living he felt oppressed by the absence of any private life—a result of existing circumstances—and talked of a surfeit of communality, of the formation of cliques, of an involuntary community (*Zwangsgemeinschaft*) with a collective style of life, and of camp psychosis. Nor did it escape him that many of the city kids were only on Hachsharah at Steckelsdorf because they, or rather their parents, saw no other possibilities for emigration and therefore put all their hopes on the Palestine Office in Berlin where the immigration certificates were issued to those *chaluzim* (pioneers) who had been selected by the respective youth leader in charge. Yet despite his reservations, Joel König conceded that Steckelsdorf was "a peaceful enclave" even in wartime, a remote refuge where "one did not see either policemen or stormtroopers."[67] This feeling, by the way, of living on an island within a brown sea was not restricted to Steckelsdorf. It was also apparent to the trainees at the non-Zionist training farm Gross-Breesen, and—as late as 1941—at the Hachsharah-Kibbutz estate Neuendorf.[68] Where else in Germany would Jews have been able to celebrate the Hanukkah festival in the style in which it was celebrated at Steckelsdorf in the winter of 1941 and at Neuendorf in 1942? "The longed-for festive night has finally arrived. We light the Hanukkah candles and say the evening prayer. Supper in itself is a feast: pea soup, boiled haddock, potatoes—such things we do not often see on our plates. The cooks have even managed to conjure up a piece of apple pie for everybody. A few minutes after the meal is over the tables are removed, the enclosed porch is curtained off, in the dining room the benches are put up, and in a jiffy a happily chatting crowd is sitting on them. Finally all is quiet. The curtain rises. Next to the stage we can see a small table on which sits a box of colorfully painted paper representing a radio. Repeatedly the radio emits a station signature that has a distinct similarity to the traditional Hanukkah tune. 'Here is the Steckelsdorf broadcasting station,' the announcer begins. 'We bring you now the latest news from the farm.'"[69]

The celebration of the Neuendorf trainees the following year was more somber, on account of the general situation. "This year Hanukkah seemed to be more than ever a festival of struggle. We prepared it very carefully, which helped us to concentrate strongly on Jewish history. . . . We put together a colorful picture book that showed, under the heading 'Fighters,' scenes from the whole of Jewish history where Jews, in one way or other, had to do battle against the world around them. At the end everybody in the hall rose spontaneously and, for the first time in the annals of Neuendorf, broke into the Zionist hymn *Hatikvah*."[70]

At the time when the Hanukkah festival was being celebrated at Steckelsdorf and Neuendorf, that segment of German Jewry still living in Germany found itself in a state of progressive disintegration. It had all begun with the operation (*Aktion*) against the Jews on November 9-10, 1938, a pogrom organized by both party leaders and state officials that, in popular lingo, came to be known as Crystal Night (*Kristallnacht*). With its significance thus minimized, it has gone down as such in history. Its immediate cause was the assassination of a German embassy official in Paris, Legationsrat Ernst vom Rath, by a 17-year-old Polish Jew, Herschel Grynspan, who had fled from Germany not long before this event. By way of retaliation, Nazi party members and stormtroopers throughout the Reich, including recently annexed Austria, wrecked and ransacked Jewish stores as well as private homes and destroyed most of the synagogues by setting them on fire. Simultaneously, the Gestapo arrested about 30,000 Jewish men over 18 years old, imprisoned them in the concentration camps Dachau, Buchenwald, and Sachsenhausen, and did not release them again until they had given written pledges that they would leave the country permanently within the shortest possible time.[71]

Shortly before this disaster hit, one of the leaders of a by then already dissolved "assimilationist" youth group, the "Ring," wrote an assessment of the devastating situation of especially those young Jews then 16 and 17 years of age who were not, or were no longer, either associated with a youth group—and only Zionist groups were still in existence—or working on training farms in preparation for emigration.[72] Most of them, the author stated, came either from Jewish lower-middle-class homes or from formerly well-to-do families who, in consequence of progressive impoverishment, had dropped to a lower socioeconomic level. The great majority lived in urban centers, notably in Berlin. The personal lives of these young people were dismal, both current and in regard to their prospects for the future.

For one thing, the traditional Jewish stronghold, the family, was rapidly disintegrating and in many instances had become ineffective in providing a real home for the young, giving them true moral support, or transmitting values that would guide them in those troubled times. As the fathers were caught up in the relentless economic pressures exerted upon their dwindling business activities by party and state, they often lost heart and, in the evenings after work, revealed to their families what in fact they had become—broken men. Indecision, fear, frustration, all these led to endless bickering between the parents and thereby made the home for their children a place to be avoided, to be fled. One of the most frequently heard complaints that came from the sons and daughters of Jewish families was the outcry: "I cannot stand being at home anymore!"[73]

Furthermore, because of the fathers' dwindling incomes, the home had often shrunk in size as families moved from large, or at least comfortable, residences into much smaller ones. Crowded quarters were usually the result. This meant among other things that children who had had a room of their own in the past now no longer enjoyed this privilege, thereby losing their privacy, particularly painful at the age of puberty. Where did they go when they were not at home? Many of them no longer attended school, and of these the lucky ones had found some sort of job, by then nearly always in a Jewish-owned enterprise. And for the most part it was just that, a job, not a vocation truly wanted or desirable. The remainder simply drifted. But there were few places left where they could "drift." By 1938 most general cultural forums such as concert halls or theaters had become progressively inaccessible to Jews; aside from the Jewish Cultural Association that catered to adults, there remained only a few Jewish sport clubs, which were dominated by a somewhat older generation, some ice parlors, Jewish dance halls, and the movies.

In consequence, there was widespread apathy among the young, a state of mind that also impeded their preparations for emigration, which was then a full-time job. In contrast to their peers fortunate enough to be either on Hachsharah or in Gross-Breesen, those urban-based youngsters had virtually nothing left that they could hold on to. As the author of this assessment concluded: "These youths live without a fatherland . . . , without a family or home . . . , without a [positive] attitude toward their own lives . . . , without a sense of the past . . . , without faith . . . , and without future."[74] To remedy the situation, he suggested, more efforts would have to be made to find effective ways of helping the young emigrate overseas. It was sound advice, but time was running out.

For at the end of 1938, with the November pogrom, began the definite dissolution of all remaining traces of Jewish self-administration, all communal life, all congregational activities, including religious services—in short, the end of every remnant of the autonomy that German Jewry had still been permitted to exercise. The first measures were the decrees of November 12, 1938, by which Germany's Jews were communally assessed one billion Reichsmarks as an "atonement" for vom Rath's assassination and, at the same time, were henceforth excluded from Germany's economic life. After barely a century and a half of emancipation, the German Jews were compelled, literally overnight, to choose between leaving the country or staying, completely impoverished and deprived of their civil rights, in a hostile environment—their former homeland—to await an uncertain future. In the last report (*Arbeitsbericht*) issued by the Reichsvertretung, which in July 1939 was officially renamed Reichsvereinigung der Juden in Deutschland (National Association of Jews in Germany), the situation was depicted with laconic precision:

The Jewish communities in Germany in future are to function as branches of the National Association (*Reichsvereinigung*). Thereby a communal responsibility has been imposed upon German Jewry for the final stage of its liquidation [as a communal body]. . . . Over and against this organizational settlement must be seen the by now complete exclusion of the Jews from the [German] economic and cultural spheres; the levy of an "atonement payment" (*Sühneabgabe*) at the rate of 20 percent of all Jewish property up to the sum of one billion [Reichsmarks]; far-reaching restrictions of the ways in which Jews may use their assets; . . . the exclusion of Jewish children from all public schools; the financial support of the needy primarily by the Jewish welfare agency, and only if supplementation is required by public relief. Henceforth, the Jews in Germany will be entirely on their own and must try with their strength alone to help as many people as possible to emigrate.[75]

For Jewish youth it now became more urgent than ever to leave Germany as soon as possible. To be sure, nobody at the time could have foreseen the actual course of the "Jewish Question," that is, its culmination in the "Final Solution." But the already existing and subsequently ever-increasing restrictions rendered their situation untenable. Simply the facts that now the last Jewish boys and girls still in public schools had to leave them and that there were no longer enough Jewish schools to take up the slack because of the steadily declining financial contributions from the rapidly shrinking Jewish communities were compelling enough to emigrate. "The question was not whether we would emigrate to America but rather when we could emigrate," recalls a Jewish woman originally from Nuremberg who at the time was 15 years old. And a man from Breslau, who was then 17, stated later: "After *Kristallnacht* everything changed. My mother and . . . grandfather both realized that they had to get out of Germany if possible or at least get us, my brother and myself, out."[76]

Although the opportunities for emigration of Jews had improved in no fundamental way—during the international conference at Evian in July 1938, no progress had been made in persuading the participating nations to accept more German Jews— a veritable flight out of Germany set in between Crystal Night and the outbreak of the Second World War.[77] This was partly facilitated by the fact that in response to the pogrom a number of Germany's neighboring states opened their borders to Jewish refugees, especially to youngsters, at least for a short time. In addition, those Jews who until then had hesitated to leave put now all their energies into emigration projects. At the end of 1938, there were still approximately 297,000 self-defined Jews (*Glaubensjuden*) in Germany, not counting annexed Austria. When war broke out in September 1939, there were still 185,100. In the course of six years, from the beginning of 1933, with still approximately 525,000 Jews in Germany, until 1938, roughly 228,000 Jews had emigrated. But in the ten months from November 1938 until early September 1939, another 112,000 left. This was the reaction to the blow that Crystal Night had dealt to the German Jews.[78]

As to the emigration of young Jews, only estimated figures are extant, and the available statistics list differing age groups. The following figures are based on the findings of Salomon Adler-Rudel.[79] According to those data, 116,961 Jewish youths, ranging in age from 6 to 25 years, were living in Germany in June 1933. In January 1938, only 67,200 were left in this age group; and in December 1938, of those who were then between 6 and 20 years old, 42,300 were left. In September 1939, the figure for the age group 0 to 24 years was 24,700, and on July 31, 1941 those between 0 and 18 years numbered 20,669, although not all of them were *Glaubensjuden*, i.e., bona fide adherents to the Jewish faith.

Of those young Jews who had been trained at special facilities in agriculture, handicrafts, and housework, 18,457 emigrated between April 1933 and April 1938. In addition, other youngsters left the country between 1933 and 1939—a few even as late as 1941—either with their parents or by means of special children's transports, organized by the Reichsvertretung. Between 1933 and the middle of November 1938, 1,197 Jewish boys and girls emigrated in this fashion. And between March and the end of June, 1939, another 2,623 up to age 15 left the country with children's transports, while an additional 1,700 left either with their parents or in other individual ways.[80]

Numbers, however, cannot really give a true picture of the emotional scenes that could be witnessed for years at German railway stations and the docks of overseas steamship companies. "Young people, obviously destined for Palestine, were leaning out of railway compartment windows. On the platform stood their fathers and mothers. The painful despair of the farewells that was reflected in the faces of these people was so moving, so impressive, that I have never forgotten this scene."[81] One woman reminisced in 1978: "On May 3, 1939, I was sent with a children's transport to Scotland. . . . My parents took me, their 16-year-old only daughter, to the train station in Nurnberg. The waiting for the train, the saying good-by, the pervasive thought that I would never see them again, those first few minutes on that train. . . . "[82] Here the reminiscence breaks off, in all likelihood because it had become too painful. But once the usually terrible parting was over, the feeling of freedom and, above all, safety outweighed everything else. This is what a 19-year-old girl from Worms, who in 1940 had moved with her parents to Heidelberg and from there, in October 1940, had been sent to the French detention camp Gurs as a result of the Baden mass deportations, entrusted to her diary on May 17, 1941: "Dear God, I thank You . . . that You led us out of that witches' cauldron. Yes, we are really in Lisbon. Truly, it is not a dream. We are free. We are in fairyland. Finally, finally we made it. . . . Now I can write what I want to without being afraid that it might be censored."[83]

How many lucky ones reached freedom will probably never be accurately established. If one accepts the estimate that on July 31, 1941 there were still 20,669 Jewish children aged 0 to 18 years, and 35,748 Jews aged 18 to 45 years in Germany (not counting Austria), and that within the latter group an estimated 5,000 were between the ages of 18 and 25, then approximately 26,000 young Jews still lived in Germany two months before Himmler's ban of Jewish emigration.[84]

And yet, efforts to help Jewish youth to emigrate even after war had broken out continued unabated. To be sure, the borders of nearly all Germany's neighbors had been closed since September 1939. Legal immigration into Palestine had come nearly to a complete halt as a result of British restrictive policies throughout the second half of the 1930s; and emigration overseas, be it to the North American continent, Latin America, Asia, or Africa, was possible for relatively few people. Only Shanghai was an exception and, until 1941, remained the last available refuge for thousands of German Jews.[85]

As far as Palestine was concerned, the Jewish organizations did not give up their efforts, up to the last moment, to continue with their emigration policy of the past. If the legal way to get there was narrowly restricted, there was also an illegal way: Aliyah Beth. The Palestine Office and Hechaluz chartered ships of usually dubious nationality and even more dubious seaworthiness—not to mention the crew—which usually sailed from Italian, Greek, or Yugoslav ports and, in return for lots of money, assumed the risk of smuggling Jewish chaluzim through the very alert British coastal control and then putting them ashore in Erez Israel. Until October 1, 1941, thus up to the ban of Jewish emigration from Germany, such illegal immigration into Palestine was supported by the Gestapo. Conditions on the overcrowded ships were terrible. There was often open animosity between the Jews and the crew, and the food was nearly always extremely poor. Only people hardened through Hachsharah and idealistically motivated could survive such a journey, which, with many delays, usually took two to three months to complete. Yet in this way it proved possible to get a considerable number of young Zionists through Aliyah Beth into Palestine.[86]

The great majority of those who found themselves still in Germany on October 1, 1941 however, were doomed to perish.[87] At the beginning of that year the Palestine Office, which up to that moment had organized emigration, was dissolved and its personnel transferred to the Reichsvereinigung. In March, all German Jews became subject to "obligatory labor duty," forced labor, and in the fall the definitive decree to this effect was issued.[88] In mid-1941 came the prohibition of any further occupational training for Jews, and the Reichsvereinigung was forbidden to grant any more financial support to emigration training facilities. Most of the smaller ones were dissolved, and their staffs and trainees transferred to a few of the larger ones. Thus, the Neuendorf estate served as a reception camp for boys and girls from such Hachsharah centers as Ahrensdorf, Havelberg, Jessen, and Schniebinchen. Other training centers, among them Steckelsdorf, Ahlem, and Gross-Breesen, remained operative for the time being. Yet they no longer served as occupational training centers but developed rapidly into forced labor camps where the Jewish inmates were subject to control by the regional labor offices. The latter decided how many people were to work on the estate proper, how many were farmed out to work on other large agricultural properties or at neighboring peasant holdings, in horticultural enterprises and tree nurseries, but also at railroad construction jobs, laying cables, or in factories. Although evening courses were continued whenever possible, they had to be largely restricted because, on the one hand, working hours were constantly extended, and on the other hand the food allotted to Jews was insufficient to allow the hard-working, undernourished youngsters to concentrate on intellectual matters. Hunger and fatigue affected attention spans and rendered instruction in difficult subjects, such as modern Hebrew (Ivrith), virtually impossible.

Official measures foreshadowing the physical destruction of the Jews now followed one another hard and fast. On July 31, 1941, Göring issued instructions to the effect that all necessary steps be taken "for a comprehensive solution of the Jewish Question within Germany's sphere of influence throughout Europe."[89] On September 1 followed a decree ordering Jews to wear a yellow badge with a Jewish star.[90] On October 23, the head of *Amt* IV (*Gestapo*) within the Reich Main Security Office, SS Major General (*Gruppenführer*) Heinrich Müller, informed all state and party agencies concerned that, on orders of Himmler, Jews were henceforth forbidden to emigrate "without exception, for the duration of the war."[91] And on October 14 and 24, 1941, the head of the German Regular Police (*Ordnungspolizei*), SS Lieutenant General (*Obergruppenführer*) Kurt Daluege, issued orders for the deportation of Jews from the "Great German Reich" to the East.[92]

All these decrees affected the lives of those who were in Jewish emigration training centers. Reactions to the order pertaining to the wearing of the Jewish star were still far from uniform among the young people. Thus, Annelise Ora-Borinski remembers that at Neuendorf "we had a solemn roll call when we wore the yellow badge for the first time with pride."[93] But in Steck-

elsdorf people only looked at each other and, as Joel König recalls, "for the first time the optimists shut up as well."[94] Especially outside the work camps, where no communal life gave
support to the individual, the order to wear the Jewish star had
a deeply depressing effect. Children in particular did not understand why they had to wear the badge and were helpless in the
face of Nazi abuse and physical acts of violence they encountered while wearing the star.

The emigration ban raised immediate serious apprehensions.
"Was I not right when I predicted that Germany would soon
become one single concentration camps for Jews?" shouted one
trainee at Steckelsdorf after the ban became known, and he added:
"I tell you: this war we won't survive!"[95] When the deportations
began in mid-October 1941, there was near panic, for although
none of the Jews could possibly have known at the time what
awaited them in the East, it was clear to all of them that it could
not possibly be anything good. Thus, Joel König asked himself—and probably many others did as well—

> in what way did the terms "resettlement," "repatriation," and
> "deportation" differ? Or was there a difference at all? The
> offices of the Berlin Jewish Community used still another term:
> "migration" (*Abwanderung*). But what did all these terms mean?
> Nobody provided us with a clear answer, and after a while
> we grew tired of asking. But when reports of new deportations
> increased, when people were taken away from our own group,
> then the questions once again became urgent and roused us
> from our leaden lethargy.[96]

Inge Deutschkron in Berlin had similar reactions when friends
and acquaintances received questionnaires sent to all Jews selected for the next deportation transport so that they could provide the authorities with a complete inventory of their current
possessions.[97] On the Neuendorf estate extensive and intensive
discussions took place on the question whether children whose
parents had received their deportation orders (often on very short
notice), should stay in Neuendorf with their group, or join their
parents. Most of the time the decision was made to stay because

even at the end of 1941 many of the young people still had hopes of eventually being able to emigrate to Palestine. But whenever a group of chawerim (pals, comrades) decided, in some individual case, to let this or that young friend go with the parents, a solemn farewell was arranged:

> Unforgettable minutes, each time heart-wrenching over again for all those who took part in it. Everyone in work clothes, wearing overcoats and jackets, there we stood, arms around the necks of our neighbors—a few words, and then a song: *be schalom*! [go in peace] . . . . Then a last *chasak* [be strong], a last handshake with everyone who stood in the circle! — And now one had to hurry in order not to be late for work. —How gray these morning hours were!"[98]

A few individual young Jews participated in active resistance against the National Socialist regime, some from 1933, others after the outbreak of war. As it is not feasible to discuss the matter here at length, it must suffice to state that most Jewish members of the Resistance—whether they belonged to the Group Herbert Baum or the White Rose—came from the youth movement, both Zionist and non-Zionist. Many, but especially the Group Herbert Baum, participated in the Resistance under Communist leadership. Only a few survived; most were arrested in 1942–43 by the Gestapo, sentenced, and executed. The youngest victim, a woman of the Group Herbert Baum, was 19 years old when she was handed over to the executioner.[99]

For those who were not in the Resistance, the move down the road to extinction began not much later. More and more Jewish schools had been forced to close their doors once war had broken out. The Reich Minister for Science, Education, and Popular Learning declared, in agreement with the Reich Security Main Office, that as of July 1, 1942 "schooling for Jewish children by either paid or unpaid teaching staff" would end.[100] Jewish children had no more need for schools. The proverbial "class objective" (*Ziel der Klasse*), i.e., promotion to the next higher class, had lost its meaning for Jewish children once the deportations began in the fall of 1941. Those in a position to vent their hatred of Jews had a different destiny in mind for them. It had various geographic appellations, but in the end it was the same for all of them: the "Final Solution"—death.

The emigration training centers, long since degraded to forced labor camps, also gradually disappeared. On May 21, 1942, the Steckelsdorf estate was notified by the Gestapo, in writing, that except for 15 Jewish workers still needed for the operation of the farm, all others had to be ready three days hence for "resettlement." Joel König describes the still hopeful mood: "At the stairs I ran into Rifka Berger, who was the youngest of us all. 'Should I take along my report cards from school?' she asked. 'Yes, take them, just in case! After all, they are only a few sheets of paper.' Shortly before the war broke out . . . [Rifka] had lost both her parents. Her only brother was at Dachau [concentration camp]: she had never heard from him again."[101]

The horticultural school Ahlem was closed on July 30, 1942. Until January 1944 it served as a collection center from which the deportation trains left that ultimately hauled away the Jewish citizens from the administrative districts Hanover and Hildesheim. Among the deportees were the trainees and apprentices who had still been in Ahlem when it closed down.[102]

By early spring—the end of February to early March of 1943— the last "full Jews" (*Volljuden*; according to Nazi definition, persons with two Jewish parents) had disappeared from the Jewish Emigration Training Farm Gross-Breesen, leaving only "half-Jews" behind.[103] In April the Retraining Center Paderborn and the Neuendorf estate closed down. The boys and girls from Neuendorf went first to the Gestapo collecting point Grosse Hamburger Strasse in Berlin, whence they were deported, in cattle cars, to Auschwitz. According to the report of a survivor, Polish farmers and foreign workers laboring in the fields along the tracks that led to Auschwitz drew a hand across their throat as the deportation trains passed, a gesture by which they tried to signal to the Jews heading east that they would be killed. "They did not believe it."[104]

2. Gross-Breesen Training Farm

THE FOLLOWING account of the non-Zionist emigration training farm (*Auswandererlehrgut*) Gross-Breesen intends to provide, by way of a case study,[1] a closer look into the working and living conditions of this estate. Although unique in several ways, they were nevertheless fairly representative of the occupational and pedagogical training that young Jews were then receiving at many similarly structured although overwhelmingly Zionist-run centers. The documents section that follows as chapter 3 is designed to highlight the crisis that Gross-Breesen's trainees and staff encountered in the wake of the November 1938 pogrom—"Crystal Night." The often intimate view provided by the documents of how people reacted to this crisis, in both practical and emotional terms, offers insights into what became a painful process of dissolution, dispersion and, for some, physical annihilation.

As already indicated, the passage of the Nuremberg Laws in September 1935 prompted the Reichsvertretung to explore systematically all existing opportunities for an orderly exodus of especially young Jews.[2] Around the turn of 1935–36, rumors began to circulate about plans to establish an emigration training farm for boys and girls whose ultimate destination would be a country other than Palestine, somewhere overseas. Even before these rumors had been confirmed as fact, the mere idea was attacked by the Zionist newspaper *Jüdische Rundschau* (Jewish Observer).[3] The attack centered on the non-Zionist nature of the project. "What country?" queried the author of the article. "What sort of a community mission? Representatives of which culture?" The article concluded with the dire prophecy that the whole idea

43

would be extremely harmful to the "Jewish cause." Two days after the publication of this polemic, leading members of the Reichsvertretung met in Berlin under the chairmanship of Rabbi Dr. Leo Baeck and resolved to establish just such a training farm for an initial contingent of approximately 125 boys and girls. Farming, gardening, household duties, and such crafts as carpentry and metalworking (*Schlosserhandwerk*) were the technical skills to be taught, both their theoretical and practical sides. In addition, instruction in foreign languages would be offered. Finally, character building and intensive cultivation of their spiritual and cultural heritage, notably their Jewish tradition, were to go hand in hand with the technical curriculum of the trainees. Before the meeting adjourned, its members elected a board of directors, with Dr. Julius L. Seligsohn as its chairman, and unanimously agreed to appoint as the director of the new training institute a well-known educator and social psychologist, Professor Dr. Curt Bondy. Fritz Schwarzschild was named treasurer.[4]

Curt Bondy, born in Hamburg in 1894, came of an old, established, and well-to-do Jewish merchant family. He attended a private school (*Landschulheim*), Schloss Bischofsstein, where he first came in contact with a group in the German youth movement. In 1914 he began to study medicine but had to break off when war broke out. For three years he served at the western front in the German medical corps. After the war he was one of the founders of the Sozialistische Deutsche Studentenbund (Socialist German Student League) in Hamburg, where he now studied psychology, philosophy, and public law. He obtained his doctorate under the guidance of the well-known psychologist William Stern. For two years, from 1921 to 1923, he worked as an assistant guard (*Hilfswachtmeister*) in a prison for juvenile delinquents, Hanöfersand, an island near Hamburg in the river Elbe. There he tried to introduce pedagogically progressive prison methods, but the attempt miscarried because the other prison officials were opposed to the reform plans. Bondy then went to the University of Göttingen, where he published his qualifying thesis (*Habilitationsschrift*) in 1926. Thereafter, he became for a short time the director of a prison for juvenile delinquents in

Eisenach but then accepted an invitation to go to the University
of Göttingen as an Associate Professor (*Honorarprofessor*) of
Social Pedagogy. In 1933 he was dismissed from the university
because he was a Jew. Together with Martin Buber he then worked
for the Jüdische Hilfswerk (Jewish Aid Agency) in Frankfurt/
Main. From there he went to Berlin in the spring of 1936 as
newly appointed director of the projected emigration training
center, assisted the Reichsvertretung to search for a suitable farm,
and proceeded to select future trainees from among the applicants.[5]

The spring of 1936 was taken up with negotiations between
the Reichsvertretung and the governmental agencies concerned,
notably the Reich Ministry of the Interior and the Ministry of
Agriculture. Official permission to lease the needed facilities for
a training center was granted, in principle, without delay but
remained subject to final approval by both ministries once a suitable farm had been found.[6] At this point, on February 20, 1936,
the business office of the Jewish emigration training farm-to-be
invited boys and girls between the ages of 15 and 17, and training assistants (*Praktikanten*) between the ages of 17 and 23, to
send in their applications for admission.[7] Meanwhile, the active
search for a suitable facility continued and lasted until the middle
of April, when the Reichsvertretung succeeded in leasing an estate in Silesia, Gross-Breesen. It was owned by a Jewish family,
Rohr. The Rohrs were of Polish nationality, had returned to Poland in 1933, and were willing to put their estate at the disposal
of the Reichsvertretung rent-free.[8]

Gross-Breesen, situated about 30 kilometers north of Breslau
(today Wroclaw) in the district of Trebnitz, near Obernigk, had
once been a nobleman's estate (*Rittergut*). It encompassed 567
acres of farmland, meadows, woods, and buildings. With its
slightly rolling landscape, its beautiful stand of woods surrounding many of the fields and meadows, and the large manor house
(*Schloss*) standing above and somewhat apart from the farmyard
with its stables and the rather primitive dwellings of the permanent farmworkers (*Instleute*), it offered an ideal location for
a training center. The very fact that it was somewhat rundown

increased the challenge and possibilities for the prospective trainees, who were given the opportunity to transform a fairly neglected estate into a productive, going concern.[9]

Before the gates of Gross-Breesen could be officially opened,
a good deal of local opposition had to be overcome. The district
administrator (*Landrat*) in Trebnitz and the local party head
(*Kreisleiter*) voiced strong protests against a "Jew farm" (*Ju-
dengut*) in their bailiwick, and negotiations dragged on until the
end of April when the last objections were finally overcome. By
the time the first trainees arrived at Gross-Breesen in May 1936,
a complete staff had been recruited and was ready to get to work.
Aside from the director, Curt Bondy, who assumed the overall
guidance, the agricultural training was entrusted to Chief Manager (*Oberinspektor*) Erwin Scheier. His wife, Ruth, supervised
the household and the training of the girls. Master Carpenter
(*Meister*) Max Kiwi, who arrived with his family shortly after
the opening of Gross-Breesen, set up a carpentry shop with modern machinery and was responsible for this aspect of specialized
training. He was ably assisted in this task by his son, Hermann,
who held a carpenter's journeyman diploma. Traute Meyer acted
as secretary to Bondy and handled all official paperwork. Finally, a former government building officer (*Baurat*) dismissed
as a Jew after 1933, R. Jacoby, though not a permanent member
of the staff, spent many weeks on the premises in order to re-
model and furnish the manor house, where the majority of the
staff and trainees had their quarters.[10]

Even before a final decision had been made as to the location
of the training center, throughout March and early April, a small
staff under Bondy's supervision had begun to screen the numerous applicants, of whom only a little more than one hundred
could be admitted. Standards for admission were high. A sound
body and mind as well as good character were the chief prereq-
uisites in the selection process.[11] Whenever possible, Bondy in-
terviewed each applicant in person, and in the last analysis pre-
ferred someone with a slight health defect over one whose character
seemed doubtful. For whereas some adjustment could be made
for the former, a trainee with character deficiencies could
become a danger to the community that was to be built at the

training farm. The selection process proved highly successful; subsequently only a very few persons had to be expelled from Gross-Breesen and most of them for minor infractions. Applications of boys vastly outnumbered those of girls during the initial screening process. To correct the situation, Bondy toured a number of cities later in 1936 and pleaded with the parents in the Jewish communities to send their girls to Gross-Breesen. The appeal, however, was only moderately successful, and no satisfactory balance of the sexes was ever achieved.[12]

At the time when the decision was taken to found a non-Zionist agricultural training farm for Jewish boys and girls, the question of the nature of the training naturally arose at once. That a thorough familiarization with agricultural theory and practice had to be given primary attention was, of course, self-evident. But was such training in itself sufficient to prepare the young people properly for a new life in an alien environment? Both the Reichsvertretung and Bondy agreed that mere practical training was not enough. It would have to be supplemented by an educational approach designed to meet also the spiritual, emotional, and cultural needs of the future settlers. In short, there was consensus among the founders of Gross-Breesen that character building and the inculcation of spiritual and cultural values were as important as the teaching of technical skills. Only thus could the danger of proletarianization (*Verbauern*) be forestalled.[13] The details on how to deal with this phase of education were not spelled out, however, but were largely left to the discretion of Curt Bondy.

The newly appointed director of Gross-Breesen faced the task of gathering a group of youngsters who ultimately were expected to settle as a group at some destination overseas. A first contingent, it was hoped, should emigrate comparatively soon to a still-to-be-found country anywhere in the world, and there establish a bridgehead, so to speak, for subsequent groups of Gross-Breesen youths that were to follow in due time once they had completed their training. As it had been resolved by the Reichsvertretung that all boys and girls, in addition to being taught occupational skills, were to be introduced to subjects pertaining to their German and Jewish heritage, Bondy made the nontechnical aspects

of the training program his main function. In this he was later
aided by one of the training assistants, Ernst Cramer.[14] Shortly
after the first trainees had arrived, Bondy developed a concept
that he called "the three pillars" on which any future settlement
overseas would have to rest: a solid knowledge of farming methods; a conscious affirmation of Jewish tradition; and an appreciation of those aspects of German culture that transcended the
then prevailing pollution of Nazi "ideology" and practice. A fourth
pillar, although never formally included in this metaphorical
construct, proved actually the most vital aspect of Bondy's educational approach. It was his systematic attempt to convey to
his charges a set of moral precepts by which he expected them
to be governed while at Gross-Breesen and in their future life
overseas.[15] During weekly discussion meetings, usually held on
Saturday mornings, he conducted what he called "Knowing Life"
sessions, or *Lebenskunde* (approximately, guide on how to live
and behave; rap session). Each of these sessions dealt with a
specific theme that either grew out of Bondy's general observations during the week or developed from a particular incident
that had taken place during the workaday life of the community.
The topics tended to range widely, and although the incident that
inspired them was usually insignificant by itself, Bondy's subsequent use of it was not. Thus, complaints from the farm's chief
manager, Erwin Scheier, that there was too much talking during
work in the fields led to a session on "when to talk and when
to be silent" (*Reden und Schweigen*). Once, after rolls of toilet
paper were found scattered and trampled underfoot because people were too lazy to attach them to their proper fixtures, that
week's discussion dealt with "the individual's responsibility toward the community." Other themes treated were "attitudes toward one's work," "use of spare time," and "relations between
boys and girls," whereby it was clearly understood that sexual
abstinence for all adolescents—and most trainees were—was one
of Gross-Breesen's "iron laws."[16] There were numerous other
topics, but running like a red thread through all these discussions
was Bondy's stress on self-awareness (*Bewusstmachung*) or, as
it would be called today, "consciousness raising." Whether in
personal conversation or during the weekly sessions, he always

returned to this concept as *the* essential thing to learn, so that wiseacres tended to refer behind his back to Bondy's "categorical imperative"; but self-awareness was for him indeed one of the most important aspects of education, notably self-education. What he meant by this term was the individual's persistent efforts to recognize his or her own shortcomings and prejudices and, by this conscious act of becoming aware of such weaknesses, to fight and ultimately overcome them.[17] In view of the importance that he attached to self-awareness, Bondy expected every trainee to scrutinize his or her behavior at all times in order to determine whether it was in accordance with the ethical and moral standards of the Breesen community. Whatever else the group may *not* have learned during those years, this particular point nobody ever forgot.[18]

All these efforts had only one aim: to develop in each boy and girl strong, healthy character traits that were needed to build a sound human foundation for the envisaged future settlement abroad. In the last analysis it was therefore deemed more important that the trainees be honest and responsible people than that they could milk six cows in an hour by hand. And they responded to this approach with alacrity, in part because most of its facets were familiar to them. For Gross-Breesen's standards of behavior and educational methods were by and large those of the youth movement and the private progressive schools (*Landschulheime*) of the Weimar period. Not only Bondy himself but a large number of trainees as well came from this background, particularly from the youth movement, and the attitudes and views that they had absorbed in the youth groups helped them to adjust to their new environment with relative ease. As a result, Gross-Breesen was to them from the outset much more than merely an institution designed to teach them farming methods, carpentry, housework, etc., but became an intensive and meaningful personal experience, the strength of which outlasted the project as such by half a century. Indeed, the esprit de corps, self-respect, and high level of maturity that prevailed in the Breesen community was rarely lost on visitors from the outside.[19] They were frequently members of the Reichsvertretung, notably Otto Hirsch, Julius Seligsohn, Alfred Hirschberg, Fritz Schwarzschild, and others, all of whom looked upon Gross-Breesen with the interest, pride, and concern of "founding fathers," which, in fact, they were.

As already stated, character building figured so prominently in Gross-Breesen's educational scheme, was held to be so fundamental and all pervasive, that Bondy did not even count it specifically among the "pillars" on which a future settlement was to be based. But the pillars, too, had to be built, and every effort was made to give equal weight to all major phases of training. Of these, the agricultural part proved least problematic. To be sure, most of the boys and girls were novices when it came to farming techniques. They generally came from urban middle-class homes and had rarely, if ever, seen a cow barn from the inside. Everything was new to them; everything had to be learned from scratch. For this reason they had to attend classes in agricultural techniques and theories in addition to the practical work that they did in the fields and stables. The classes were conducted by either Chief Manager Scheier or by one of the older training assistants, some of whom had acquired prior farming experience elsewhere. Animal husbandry, crop rotation, the use of fertilizers and manure, the different growing cycles of cereals, fruits, grasses, vegetables, potatoes, and beets were all carefully studied and discussed. Classes were supplemented by field trips around the estate, conducted by Erwin Scheier. It was not always easy for the chief manager to impart his knowledge to young people who came for the most part from an urban environment. Whereas Bondy tended to stress self-awareness, Scheier urged his pupils to learn how to observe, how to "get a feel" for the wonders of nature, how to distinguish rye from barley, winter wheat from summer wheat, sugar beets from turnips. He taught them how to use a hay fork properly, how to drive a tractor, and whatever else was essential knowledge for future farmers. The majority of trainees caught on rather fast, however, and the "veterans"—some of two weeks', some of two months' standing, or longer—would make gentle fun of new arrivals who, in the terminology of the group, still had to develop from clumsy "Ottos" (the origin of the term defies investigation) into seasoned milkers, hay wagon loaders, or hoers of potatoes.

When Gross-Breesen opened its doors in the first week of May 1936, living accommodations were still rather primitive, and everything, including the work schedule, was improvised throughout the month. There were no beds, no wardrobes, no showers. Trainees slept on the floor, lived out of suitcases, and took bucket baths. An early visitor, Paul Yogi Mayer, formerly the leader of the by then disbanded Jewish youth group "Black Troop" (Schwarzes Fähnlein, Jungenschaft), some of whose former members were now Breesen trainees, wrote about his impressions in *Der Schild* (The Shield), the organ of the Jewish War Veterans (*RjF*):

Waking time is 5 A.M., and sleepy-eyed figures stumble over the scattered buckets and pipes of the plumbers to wash themselves clean and awake. Then the bedding is straightened, people get dressed, and everybody goes down for breakfast, which consists of bread and oatmeal—everywhere a proven basis for a working day.

Formation is held on the grass of the park, and boys and girls are given their work assignments for the day. Then it is off to the fields. One of the training assistants, already experienced in agriculture, drives a team of cows [they were oxen, of course—author] from one pile of weeds and rocks to the next to cart them off after the boys had gathered them together. Others are assigned to the carpentry shop, where the master carpenter is busy turning an old horse barn into a modern workshop. A few semi-invalids and boys capable of helping in the office are assigned to the house, others to the garden, and the remainder help with plastering over cracks in the walls [of various buildings]. . . .[20]

As time went on, the structure of the working day became more standardized—as much as agricultural work can ever be standardized, given the changing weather conditions—and a certain routine had developed in the first few weeks after Gross-Breesen became operational. By mid-June, double-decker bunks and wardrobes had arrived, showers had been installed, but the waking time remained unchanged: 5 A.M. in the summer, an hour or an hour and a half later in wintertime. Unchanged also remained the early morning washing procedure, although the bucket baths were replaced by cold showers; only on Friday nights could the trainees take hot showers, before the beginning of the Sabbath services. Breakfast remained simple, just as Mayer had witnessed it, and more often than not the porridge or farina were burned because the girl trainees working in the kitchen had to learn how to cook on a coal stove in huge containers designed for a hundred-odd hungry mouths. As Bondy presided over breakfast nearly every morning, none of the complaints voiced—and few dared voice any—persuaded him to permit anybody *not* to eat the burned meal. Discipline, notably self-discipline, was writ large. Morning formation also continued as long as Breesen existed as a training farm. As in the army, boys and girls lined up in two ranks by size, the tallest on the right, the smallest on the left. All the girls stood together on the far left of the second rank—indicative of the fact that they really did not quite measure up to the boys in importance. After Scheier had given everybody his or her assignment, the various groups and/or individuals proceeded to their respective places of work. Around 10 A.M., "second breakfast" was served in the field, lugged out by some of the girls in huge baskets and covered pitchers. The fare consisted usually of rye bread with jam, and "coffee" made from barley, which tasted as exciting as it sounds. Around noon, everybody would return to the manor house, where all the trainees and most of the staff lived, ate, and slept, and where all common activities took place as well, to eat lunch in the main dining hall. Here, each group composed of either boys or girls sharing one of the several dormitory-style rooms sat together at mealtimes around one of the long tables and, before starting to eat, performed in unison some odd ritual with their knives and forks accompanied by "humorous" chants. This routine, which always startled visitors, was a carryover from the youth movement. Then everybody had to go to his or her room for an hour's rest—no talking was permitted during this hour—and work would resume thereafter for the rest of the day. In the evening the columns of trainees would walk back from their various places of assignment on the estate, tired, dirty, and glad that it was *Feierabend,* the end of the day's labor. After another cold shower and a change of clothing, supper was served, to be followed by various activities that will be discussed below. By 9 P.M. all but the older training assistants had to be in bed, and Bondy made spot checks to make sure that there was no more talking after lights-out.

At the end of the first year, a seasoned Breesen trainee would have undergone a variety of experiences. If he was a boy, he might have started out as one of a crew during the hay harvest in June 1936, cutting, raking, and eventually unloading the hay into the loft—a dirty, dusty, hot, and dangerous job if one considers the fact that ten or more unskilled people were wielding hay forks in semidarkness and crowded quarters with feverish abandon. He might then have been assigned for six weeks to the dairy, the domain of the head milker (*Oberschweizer,* called "Ober") where the Holstein cows and the heavy, dangerous bull—which would have won first prize at a local agricultural fair in 1937 had it not come from the "Jew farm"—kept him occupied intermittently for twelve hours a day. Performance in the dairy was the yardstick by which a trainee's intrinsic suitability for farming was measured, and most of the boys as well as the few "privileged" girls assigned to this tour of duty passed the test well.[21] For a test it was, if not an ordeal. The head milker was a martinet. The barn was an archaic, probably eighteenth-century structure with very old-fashioned stalls, poor drainage, and poor light, all of which made feeding and milking—no milking machines, of course—rather difficult. The hours were long, the work hard and, given the unsanitary conditions that prevailed, unbelievably filthy. All efforts to keep animals and premises clean remained an exercise in futility. Worst of all, the absence of sanitation affected the trainees assigned to dairy duty very directly. Even after a shower—"warm" every day for this particular brotherhood—and a change of clothes, the stench of the barn clung to every member of the crew during the entire tour of dairy training. As a result, every one of them was politely avoided by the rest of the Breesen community.

Having successfully survived this phase of the program, a typical trainee would then participate in the grain harvest with all its numerous chores. Putting up sheaves while walking behind the horse-drawn harvester, loading the dry sheaves onto wagons, unloading the wagons in the barn, and stacking the sheaves neatly and at top speed, all this would occupy him until the end of the harvest when the last load was brought in—an event accompanied by shouting, singing, and a general feeling of accomplishment. It was during the harvest of 1936 that the boys and girls at Gross-Breesen really grew into a community. The bickering that had still been very much in evidence throughout the haying season ceased. The trainees began to show pride in their work and thought nothing of working overtime, sometimes by moonlight, if a given field had to be finished. Such decisions were made spontaneously, without the prodding of either Scheier, his "Aryan" deputy Herr Gamrot, or the foreman (*Schaffer*) of the regular farmhands (*Instleute*) of the estate. Although the latter worked side by side with the trainees in the fields, contacts between the two groups were, for political reasons, carefully restricted to working hours. And even during working hours this separation was maintained whenever possible because some of the farmhands were members of the Nazi Party, and all of them were "Aryans."

Between the end of the grain harvest and the onset of winter lay another heavy stretch of work. Seemingly endless rows of potatoes, sugar beets, and turnips had to be taken out of the ground before frost set in. As in all other harvests, boys and girls worked side by side, often in driving rain and cold wind that turned their gloveless hands reddish-blue and numb. For wearing gloves during work, regardless of the weather conditions, was frowned upon by the supervising powers, presumably because they considered this Spartan rule part of a necessary toughening-up process.

After the fruits of the earth had been gathered and stored, long lines of shivering figures trudged across the empty, muddy fields with wire baskets in their hands to pick up rocks and stones and dump them in piles by the side of the fields. With the coming of winter, working hours were somewhat shortened, but not much. Straw mats with which to cover hotbeds had to be woven. Rye, wheat, barley, and oats were threshed in an old threshing machine that tended to break down periodically. Ice for the ice house, where the milk was stored in cans during the summer months, had to be sawed on the frozen pond behind the stables. Potatoes were sorted in cold and musty cellars by the light of kerosene lamps; and, finally, some trees were cut in the woods, their trunks to be sold for timber, their branches piled high next to the communal baking oven in which bread was baked all year round.

In addition to those general chores that were performed by everybody who was available, some individuals were selected for specialized training in particular branches of agriculture. Thus, physically frail trainees were frequently assigned to truck gardening, a designation that earned them the epithet *Schmalspurlandwirte* (literally, narrow-gauge farmers). The chickens and all other small domestic animals, including the pigs that had to be carefully screened off from visiting dignitaries of the Breslau Jewish community, were likewise entrusted to only a few chosen boys and girls who rapidly developed into "experts." The same held true for the operation of the antediluvian tractor. A few privileged characters, for the most part training assistants, were allowed to drive the teams of horses, but their supervision remained on the whole the prerogative of some of the regular farmhands.

Just as nearly everybody underwent training in the dairy barn and worked throughout the seasons in the fields, a six-week carpentry course in Meister Kiwi's shop was also mandatory; so was a tour of duty in the farm's blacksmith shop. The girls, always a somewhat neglected minority at Gross-Breesen, were given as much opportunity as possible to work on the outside, but their household training received priority. Under Ruth Scheier's guidance they did the cooking, baked bread, cleaned house, did laundry (by hand, of course!), mended endless pairs of torn socks, and did some canning. Throughout its existence, Gross-Breesen was a bustling antheap of ceaseless activity, most of which was hard, serious work. It was indeed a remarkable measure of success that the estate, which had initially operated at a loss, was self-supporting by June 1938.[22]

Whereas the occupational training in all its phases posed hardly any serious problems, attempts to give the trainees an equally intensive cultural education were by and large condemned to fail-

ure. It has been mentioned that the founders of Gross-Breesen
wanted to impart to the future settlers overseas at least a firm
cultural foundation in Judaism and German literature, music, etc.
But although there was no lack of good intentions on everybody's part, the two pillars pertaining to nonoccupational training never quite attained supporting strength. Perhaps the most
decisive factor in this development was time pressure. Since it
was always a real possibility that the Nazi authorities might de-
cide to close the training center between one day and the next,
the acquisition of theoretical and practical farming skills, so essential for each individual trainee, assumed primary importance,
while cultural activities were largely relegated to Saturdays, Sundays, and occasional short periods on weekday evenings. But
since weekends were also reserved for theoretical instruction in
farming techniques, foreign language classes, and recreational
activities, little time was left for much else.

Despite these difficulties, however, everything possible was
done to stimulate interest especially in classical music, literature,
and current events. Every day ended with a brief musical performance, either by a trio of trainees or, often, by Bondy at the
piano. Attendance was voluntary; but on Sunday nights all trainees were expected to be at the hour-long concert which, tradi-
tionally, was performed at that time. There were other events as
well. A play-reading group presented Lessing's *Nathan der Weise*
(Nathan the Sage); the musicologist Karl Adler visited for a two-
day singing session; and Bondy read aloud from some significant
works of world literature. Twice a week the trainees were briefed
on current events, and everybody was encouraged to read newspapers, which were available to all in the assembly room. In
addition, the various groups of boys and girls—the "families"
rooming together within the Breesen community—met at least
one evening a week in their respective rooms for activities and
discussions best suited for each individual group. Here, too, works
of fiction or poetry were read aloud, records were played, or
songs—generally from the youth movement—were sung to the
accompaniment of guitars. Two highpoints of cultural activity
were a visit by Martin Buber, who led a general discussion on
the theme "Love thy neighbor, for he is like thee," and a very

impressive outdoor performance of Beer-Hofmann's *Der junge David* (The Young David) by a large cast of Breesen boys and girls.

To be sure, such occasions left a deep impression and were greatly appreciated, but in the last analysis they were predominantly recreational and were no substitute for an intensive humanistic education. The latter the majority of the trainees lacked, because their formal schooling had, in most cases, been prematurely terminated by the adverse political circumstances. Such explanation, however, is inadequate to explain why Gross-Breesen failed to generate within its community that positive affirmation of Judaism originally envisaged by the Reichsvertretung.

What were the reasons? One of the most fundamental was the personal background of the trainees. A large number of them, probably the majority, came from assimilated middle-class Jewish families who belonged to either liberal or reform congregations. In some instances they belonged to none at all, which was usually the case with parents of a mixed marriage. Although many of the trainees had been members of the German-Jewish youth movement, only a handful among them had acquired there a marked religious outlook, unless they already possessed it when they joined. Those who came to Gross-Breesen as indifferent Jews, at best as "three-day Jews" who throughout the year observed only the high holidays of Rosh Hashanah (two days), and Yom Kippur, and this because of convention rather than from inner religious conviction—these eventually left Gross-Breesen with their sentiments unchanged.[23] The very fact that they chose to go to a non-Zionist emigration training center where, after lengthy initial debates, food was not kosher and religious practices were both liberal and minimal determined to a great degree both the composition and the attitude of the community. To create under these circumstances an atmosphere in which Judaic tradition could flourish was undoubtedly a thorny task, and it fell to Curt Bondy to cope with it.

Gross-Breesen's director, although Jewish, had not been raised in a religious household. Jewish teachings and traditions, in short the content and forms of Judaism, were alien to him. Despite this obvious handicap he tried loyally and unremittingly to foster an atmosphere of Jewish consciousness and values among all trainees, and the fact that he was as much of a "seeker" in this endeavor as they were only heightened his determination. Aided by Frau Ruth Scheier and some of the training assistants, notably Karl (Wastl) Neumeyer,[24] he embarked on an intensive program designed to make Judaism a viable part of the community.

Friday evening services were held regularly, and attendance for both boys and girls was mandatory. A few of the boys who came from religious homes took turns leading the services, which, by their very unpretentiousness, were impressive. A festive meal at decorated tables followed the services and ended with the singing of *Shir Hama'alos* (Psalm 123) by the assembled community. All Jewish holidays were celebrated in the traditional fashion of "liberal" Judaism, and throughout Gross-Breesen's existence religious instruction was given by visiting teachers and some members of the community proper. In short, there was no lack of goodwill, either on Bondy's part or on that of the trainees. Yet all these efforts did not really accomplish more than strengthening the bonds of friendship that became so pronounced during the relatively brief timespan allotted to the training farm. In other words, common worship on Friday evenings and religious holidays had the same effect as the play readings, evening concerts, and "Knowing Life" sessions; they turned the trainees into more loyal Breeseners rather than into committed Jews, except for those few who had been religious before their arrival. All these attempts at "getting religion" were emotionally stimulating experiences that emphasized the closeness of the group; but on the whole, they did not go deeper. To this must be added that the generally uninspired but mandatory religious instruction provided by visiting teachers from Breslau elicited the same unenthusiastic response as did the likewise mandatory cold showers at five o'clock in the morning. Half a year before the adult male population of Gross-Breesen was sent off to a concentration camp, Bondy admitted privately that the attempt to foster a genuine Jewish religious attitude among the trainees had failed.[25]

Because the search for a final destination was as important as the training that prepared the future settlers for emigration, exploratory steps in this direction were taken as soon as Gross-

Breesen became operative in May 1936. The main responsibility for investigating the possibilities for emigration was assumed by the Reichsvertretung, which, in this task, collaborated closely with the Hilfsverein der Juden in Deutschland (Aid Society of the Jews in Germany, established in 1901 as Hilfsverein der deutschen Juden, Aid Society of German Jews, with the task of aiding East European Jews in particular to immigrate, from Russia, via Germany to the USA).[26] Among those who cooperated most closely with Bondy in the attempt to settle Gross-Breesen's trainees overseas, three names deserve special mention: Otto Hirsch and Julius L. Seligsohn of the Reichsvertretung, both of whom paid ultimately with their lives for the devotion they showed to German Jewry in general and to Gross-Breesen in particular; and *Regierungsrat* (Government Counselor) Hermann von Freeden of the Reichsstelle für das Auswanderungswesen (roughly, Reich Emigration Office), a section of the German Ministry of the Interior in Berlin that was responsible for all matters pertaining to emigration. Von Freeden worked closely and harmoniously with the Jewish agencies, and in the course of his official functions often took personal risks to render assistance.[27]

During the first two years of Gross-Breesen's existence its emigration plans were largely conceived in terms of a communal settlement, a "New Gross-Breesen," somewhere overseas, and in the summer of 1936 all hopes along these lines were fixed on the Brazilian province of Paraná.[28] A special commission was selected by the Reichsvertretung and sent to Brazil in order to investigate the opportunities for such a project on the spot. Gross-Breesen's representative on the commission was Karl (Wastl) Neumeyer. The summer passed, the commission returned, and for the next two years negotiations with the Brazilian government continued without making any headway. In fact, until 1939 no concrete project for any group settlement, however restricted in size, materialized, and those who emigrated from Gross-Breesen before that year left on an individual basis. New projects, however, continued to appear on the horizon, all of which required extensive and painstaking negotiations.

By far the most promising of them—and ultimately the only one that was actually realized—was the so-called Virginia Plan.

In the spring of 1938, Bondy traveled to the United States in order to investigate opportunities for an agricultural settlement in that country. During the course of his visit the American Jewish Joint Distribution Committee learned of a generous Jewish department-store owner in Richmond, Virginia, William B. Thalhimer, who offered to purchase a nearby farm on which 30 Jewish refugees from Germany could be settled. By the time Bondy embarked on his return voyage to Germany, the "Joint" had begun to secure sponsors willing to provide the required affidavits, and had also taken the necessary preparatory steps with the U.S. Department of State in requesting entry permits for the Breesen trainees under a special agricultural quota.[29]

While the Paraná project with its inconclusive negotiations was eclipsed by the Virginia Plan, a third possible opportunity appeared when a section of the emigrants' aid organization HICEM, the Jewish Colonization Association (ICA), based in Paris, offered to settle 30 young Jewish farmers in groups of five on one of its colonies in Argentina.[30] As it turned out in the end, only five people altogether, two married couples and one single young man from Gross-Breesen, were able to go to the ICA colony Avigdor, and hopes that a larger contingent would follow the first group were never realized.[31] Finally, a few trainees left in 1937 and 1938 individually—some of them alone, some with their parents—for Chile, Uruguay, Argentina, Brazil, England, and the Netherlands. Two training assistants went as farmworkers to Kenya Colony, Africa; two others, under the regular immigration quota, went as pioneers to Hyde Farmlands, Virginia—the farm that meanwhile Mr. Thalhimer had purchased—while the fate of the remaining prospective Virginia settlers continued to hang in the balance. Thus, when the harvest season of 1938 was over, most boys and girls who had started their training two years earlier, and those who had been admitted since, were still in Gross-Breesen and continued to wait for permission to go to Virginia, Avigdor, or Paraná. By that time the original idea of simply transplanting the entire Breesen community to one country had been abandoned. The best that could be expected was to leave in small groups and to settle wherever an opportunity for emigration opened up.[32] This waiting period, accompanied by hopes, frustrating negotiations with consular officials of foreign countries, and recurrent disappointments ended abruptly on November 10, 1938. For the mass arrests of roughly 30,000 Jewish men throughout Germany in the wake of Crystal Night did not spare Gross-Breesen either.

The events triggered across the country by the assassination attempt on the German Legation secretary in Paris and his death two days later on November 9, 1938 were not yet known in Gross-Breesen on the morning of November 10. It was only known that there had been an assassination attempt. Newspapers did not arrive in Gross-Breesen until around noon, and since the press reports up until November 10 were rather cautious in general, it seemed that there was no cause for particular fear.[33] Bondy drove by car to his dentist in Breslau early in the morning, but turned around at once when he saw the destruction to the Jewish stores in the city and learned the reasons for it from passersby. He reached Gross-Breesen just as the arrests were commencing there.[34]

SS men in uniform drove onto the farm in two or three trucks. They were accompanied by Police Commissioner Schubert from Breslau. All the personnel—administration, staff, and trainees—were ordered to proceed to the main building, the manor house, for roll call, and the young people working the stables had to go out to the fields, accompanied by the SS, to communicate the order to the group working there. When everyone had gathered, Schubert read the names of the Jews from a list, and as soon as those called had answered, they were put into one of three groups: men 18 years or older, boys under 18 years, women and girls. Schubert, who did not appear to be a fanatic, did not keep strictly to the age limits, but rather, put four or five especially young-looking teenagers into the younger group even though they were over 18 years old (which was "corrected" by the local police the next day). Then all three groups were locked in different rooms and stayed there under SS guard until early afternoon.

After these "formalities" had been taken care of, the next point on the program came up. Probably by order of the SS, but perhaps on their own initiative, a few of the regular farmworkers went to the main building, where none of the three groups were being held. They began systematically to destroy the windows and furniture. The SS had had Master Carpenter Kiwi fetch a sledge hammer from the carpentry shop before he was led away. Armed with this and other tools, the blacksmith, the teamsters Gajek and Krause, and others went from room to room, turned over cabinets, smashed the dishes in the kitchen, broke window-panes, and in the meeting room destroyed the grand piano, a plaster reproduction of Michelangelo's Moses, the Torah cabi-net, and the Torah, which Krause hacked to pieces and threw onto the dungheap. Only Bondy's room was spared. There the SS leaders were sitting together, drinking. They were having Ruth Hadra, one of Bondy's assistants, serve them. Four "prominent" farm employees had kept their distance from the raid of destruc-tion: the foreman; the head milker (who, that same evening for the first time since the founding of the training farm, appeared in the main building to bring fresh milk to the boys who had not been taken away and had meanwhile returned there, as well as the girls); old Franzke, in his late seventies, who supervised the granary; and the coachman Stoppel, also over seventy, who oc-casionally went to the Gellendorf station with a team of horses to pick up visitors and bring them back to Gross-Breesen in grand style. Fortunately there was no abuse; nobody was physically threatened or touched. Instead, some personal property of the trainees disappeared, especially cash, and a few typewriters. Whether the thefts were committed by the SS, who "supervised" the destructive raid, or by the regular farmhands can no longer be ascertained.

Although contact between the young Breeseners and the reg-ular farmworkers since the founding of the training farm had never been intimate, it had always been peaceful and without incidents of any sort. Thus, it is very possible that the fury of destruction displayed that day was not so much directed against the Jews but rather was an eruption of long-smouldering bitter-ness that the poorly paid farmworkers who lived primitively felt against those in the manor, regardless of who they were. The main building was the former manor of a *Junker* (aristocratic Prussian estate owner), under whom their fathers, mothers, and grandparents may have worked, so for them it was a symbol of exploitation and servitude. The pogrom made it possible for them to do quite "legally" what for centuries peasants had done in all uprisings, namely, to smash the master's house to bits.

When the women and girls as well as the group under 18 (including the four or five other boys that Police Commissioner Schubert had put in this group) were released from temporary custody in the early afternoon, the third group was no longer there. Frau Scheier, Ruth Hadra, and "Prinz," one of those over 18 years old, discussed what was to be done. The telephone line had been cut, so that it was impossible to make contact with the outside world. Was Gross-Breesen now dissolved? The SS had left behind no instructions. Should the boys who had not been arrested continue working along with the girls, as if nothing had happened? Would they have problems with the authorities, above all with the Reich Food Supply Agency (Reichsnährstand), if the work at the farm were stopped without instructions from outside? These were all questions that could not be answered at that time. So they decided at the moment to clean up as much as possible. The next day, November 11, Prinz was to go to Breslau and get instructions from the state farmers association (*Landesbauernschaft*).

But things did not get that far. About midnight policemen appeared, accompanied by several stormtroopers, and arrested Prinz and the others who, thanks to Schubert's intervention, remained in Breesen. In the early afternoon of November 11 they, too, were taken away. In the process they learned that not all National Socialists took part enthusiastically in the pogrom. A stormtrooper who guarded them during the night of November 11 distanced himself notably from Dr. Goebbels' "boiling soul of the people" (*kochende Volksseele*): "You should see what they've done in Breslau," were his approximate words. "The synagogues there are burning. That is just crazy. One can also be a reasonable anti-Semite." It was only then that Prinz and his companions realized that the destruction of Gross-Breesen was not an isolated incident.[35]

While the women and youths who remained in Gross-Breesen, still confused by the events that had befallen them, made an attempt to master the new situation, which was completely unclear to them, the group of arrested men—besides Bondy, Scheier,

and Master Carpenter Kiwi, about twenty trainees—was on the
way to the Buchenwald concentration camp. Of course, they did
not know that, and they also had no idea that they were victims
of a major pogrom that on the evening of November 9 had been
ordered first by the chief of the Gestapo office in Berlin, SS
Colonel (*Standartenführer*) Heinrich Müller, and then shortly afterward by the chief of the security police and the security service (SD), SS Major General (*Gruppenführer*) Reinhard Heydrich: the arrest of 20,000 to 30,000 Jewish men in the whole
Reich and their transfer to the nearest of three respective concentration camps, Dachau, Sachsenhausen, or Buchenwald. The
Jews from Silesia were delivered to Buchenwald, where a total
of just under 10,000 *Aktionsjuden* (Jews arrested in the pogrom)
were taken into custody.[36]

A detailed report on the Buchenwald concentration camp would
overstep the boundaries of this work;[37] for our purposes let it
suffice to describe briefly the experiences of the Breesen group.
The transport to Buchenwald was similar to that in other parts
of Germany, for which there are witnesses. The trip to Breslau
in trucks proceeded without particular incident or maltreatment.
In Breslau the first stop was police headquarters, where the prisoners from all parts of Silesia had to stand in the courtyard and
were given something to eat there. The Chief Commissioner of
Police showed his human side when he sent back home about
six people badly wounded in the war, some of them on crutches.
The group that had been arrested on November 10 spent the night
in the Breslau police headquarters, where they tried to sleep on
sheets of confiscated literature. The following day the prisoners
had to march in groups to one of the two freight train stations,
accompanied by insults from a small group of people lining both
sides of the street. When they arrived there they were loaded
into passenger cars. Treatment during the trip depended on the
attitude of the guards: in some compartments things got very
loud, while in others the atmosphere remained comfortable. In
the compartment of the second Breesen group an SS man slipped
the boys chocolate when the young policeman who was accompanying the transport was not looking.[38]

The atmosphere changed abruptly, however, after arrival in

Weimar. When they were getting off at the train station, SS men and police stood on both sides of the platform and with belts, shoulder straps, and other objects whipped the captives down the stairs into the pedestrian underpass, where more uniformed men whipped them into lines. Here were the first injuries and even deaths, especially among the older and sick Jews. As shown by the reports of former non-Jewish Buchenwald prisoners, this abuse and also the continued treatment of the apprehended Jews was pure routine for the guard personnel: in Buchenwald all prisoner transports were "greeted" this way. The completely confused people were beaten onto trucks and driven through the gate bearing the inscription, "My Country, Right or Wrong," into the camp. Then came the wild chase under continuous blows down the entrance road, the so-called Karacho Way, to the main barracks. After that, conditions worsened for the *Aktionsjuden* as compared to the non-Jews and the Jews brought to Buchenwald earlier. Their detention in a separate part of the camp proved to be hell on earth. The SS crammed them into the totally overcrowded, makeshift barracks 1A to 5A. At first there was only one latrine for the almost 10,000 inmates, who in the first few days were given no water at all, and later only a little. The prisoners, deprived of all their rights, were now completely at the mercy of the SS personnel and their harassment and torture.

A few names from those weeks have remained imprinted on the memories of the Breeseners. There was, first of all, the reporting officer (*Rapportführer*), SS First Lieutenant (*Obersturmführer*) Hermann Hackmann, who was adjutant to the camp commander, SS Colonel (*Standartenführer*) Karl Koch. Hackmann was known by the nickname "Jonny." Young, arrogant, continually slapping his riding whip against his polished jackboots, he was a well-known figure in the camp. Daily his voice blared repeatedly through the loudspeaker with orders, instructions, threats: "Barracks 1A through 5A, attention!" Now and then SS Lieutenant Colonel (*Obersturmbannführer*) Arthur Rödl also showed up in the special part of the camp reserved for Jews. Rödl was the ranking officer in charge of prisoners taken into "protective custody" (*Schutzhaftlagerführer*).[39]

These prisoners were not assigned to work details, in contrast to the others; they were only temporarily in Buchenwald, although no one knew if and when he would be released. But the routine of their daily life was determined by the lower ranking noncommissioned officers of the SS, above all the SS sergeants (*Scharführer*), and the *Kapos* (foremen in charge of work parties and supervisors within the barracks), who themselves were prisoners and mainly criminals. The Breeseners learned very quickly to stay out of the way of every "superior" as much as possible, not to attract attention, and not go too near the watchtowers, since the SS man with his submachine gun on guard there often provided "entertainment" by having a prisoner, with his bare head that had been shaved upon arrival, stand at attention in the wintery cold often for hours until the guard was relieved or got tired of his nasty game. Willfulness paired with sadism and the fanatic anti-Semitism of the young men in SS uniforms who had been incited ideologically for years dominated the lives of the prisoners, which were also aggravated by poor quarters and miserable provisions. Prinz reported that on the day of his arrival when the newcomers had to stand stiffly for hours with their hands on their pants seams, SS Sergeant (*Scharführer*) Zöllner stamped on his feet a number of times for no apparent reason. Only the fact that Prinz was still wearing heavy workboots, which he had put on as a precaution in Breesen before departure, protected him from a crushed instep.[40]

"After another apocalyptic night," reports Ernst Cramer, "I was one of twelve young prisoners who had to carry the sick and dead out of the barracks into the wash house, while the others formed groups of a hundred according to height on the parade ground. When we were finished with our macabre work we were assigned to the group of one hundred with the shortest people, so that we towered over our neighbors by eight inches or more. An SS man in a flawless black uniform tried to equalize this dissymmetry by hitting us repeatedly on the head with a plank of wood. Fortunately the rasping order came over the loudspeaker, 'All Jew-birds into the barracks at once!' before the blows on our skulls could cause anything worse than a few lumps, scratches, and incessant pounding headaches."[41]

But these were only the smaller torments and harassments.

Other things were much worse: hunger and thirst, the lack of any sort of medical care, the completely inadequate sanitary facilities, and the primitive sleeping conditions. Because of insufficient space for the head, it was impossible to sit up in bed or to turn over, since at night the people lay pressed against each other like sardines (not to mention the corpses, which some discovered next to them occasionally on waking). The prisoners suffered most from the continual insults and degradation by the guards and from the spontaneous raids by the SS and the Kapos in the Jews' barracks, mostly at night, and—as in the first week after the wave of arrests—in a heavily drunken state. The helpless prisoners lying nearest to the barracks entrance were indiscriminately yanked out, robbed, beaten, and sometimes murdered. It is no wonder that many suffered nervous breakdowns or committed suicide, that the mortality rate during this pogrom was very high.[42]

For the Gross-Breesen group, Buchenwald was just as horrible an experience as it was for all other prisoners. After his release an 18-year-old described to the author a new discovery: he had sensed there for the first time how cheap his life was. The SS men had made him clearly conscious of that. However, the Breeseners enjoyed a few advantages not shared by most of the other prisoners that enabled them to withstand the four weeks of imprisonment (for some of them it was longer) without physical or lasting psychological damage. For one thing, they were all in good physical condition, hardened by the heavy farmwork and accustomed to spending long hours outdoors, even in bad weather. Even more important was the psychological support that they found in the fact that they did not have to survive as individuals in the camp, but rather as a group. Each of them brought along to the camp an inner control created by the "Breesen spirit," and Bondy saw to it that it was maintained there.

Farm Manager Scheier and Master Carpenter Kiwi did not measure up to the situation at all, so that they had to be taken care of like children; Bondy, however, after a brief nervous breakdown—he had a crying fit the first night at camp—retained leadership of the group firmly in hand. Ethical rules like self-awareness, responsibility toward other people, personal cleanliness, which all originated from Bondy's "Knowing Life" sessions, also maintained their validity especially in Buchenwald. But at the same time, he did not lose sight of the practical problems that arose from the emergency situation of camp life. Keeping the group together, and the survival of each individual within the group through preservation and strengthening of their physical and mental forces—this goal above all determined his approach. With this in mind he also permitted, insofar as the possibility presented itself (and it presented itself at various times), the most resourceful of the group to "arrange for" additional rations of bread and water, as long as they did not deprive other prisoners. Since the distribution of food in Buchenwald's "Jewish camp" was badly organized the entire time, Bondy made sure that the food rations were fairly apportioned to each person. But in other ways, too, the Breeseners helped one another as well as they could. Once one of the older training assistants was too conscientious about helping others: he was the sole prisoner among ten thousand to volunteer immediately when the SS objected to the filth in the Jewish part of the camp and called for volunteers to clean the parade ground and area surrounding the five barracks. The whole Breesen group helped him out, since the SS had threatened him with the customary 25 lashes with a cane or horsewhip[43] if the camp was not sparkling clean in one hour.

But the Breeseners were not just concerned about each other; they also took an interest in the fate of their companions in misfortune. Bondy certainly saw to it that, above all, the group functioned as a unit and adjusted to the conditions of the camp. This strengthened the survival instinct and the inner strength of the Breesen prisoners and helped them to withstand collectively the horror of those weeks, and to survive. Beyond that they tried, as well as they were able, to aid the other prisoners. Thus two members of the group daily had the task of supporting old and frail men on the way to the latrine and back, which, under the prevailing conditions, was no easy task.[44]

In the meantime relatives, friends, service agencies, and officials in Berlin, Amsterdam, and New York tried to secure emigration opportunities as fast as possible, regardless of whether they were for individuals or groups, overseas or only to a neighboring European country. The next chapter provides details. Since the wave of arrests served the overall purpose of eliminating Jews from the German economy and forcing them to emigrate, they were usually freed from the camp very quickly as soon as they could produce an entry permit for a country of emigration.[45]

To accomplish this, to be sure, those who wanted to emigrate had to endure a tough, time-consuming struggle with German and foreign officials. The inflexibility of the bureaucracy, its rigid adherence to procedure and traditional rules often proved to be malicious harassment. This red tape was unavoidable, whether individuals or groups were applying for emigration through the Reichsvertretung or the Palestine Office. Official records of good conduct and health certificates had to be furnished, tax declarations and proof of means had to be provided, although in 1939 there was hardly any more Jewish wealth, and the little there was could not be taken abroad. It frequently happened that at the same time two different authorities insisted on seeing the certificate of the other one before providing theirs. Visas, affidavits, and certificates from German officials often had deadlines, and if one of the documents did not arrive on time, the others, which had just been obtained with great difficulty, expired. Thus, this struggle for papers was similar in many respects to a lottery in which the much-desired immigration permit to a foreign country sparkled as the final prize. Whoever had at last and with good luck crossed all these hurdles then had to worry about the things he wanted and was allowed to take with him. Each object that went abroad was examined beforehand by an official, for Jews were no longer permitted to own valuables such as jewelry or silverware, let alone take them abroad. One had to pack under the watchful supervision of an official, usually from the secret police. Each object was entered on a list, and only then was the export of each single one approved, the baggage sealed, and the necessary certificate drawn up. All these steps cost time and money over and over again, and above all, they wore people down psychologically.

When the applicant for emigration finally had the necessary German papers together, he or she was still a long way from settling the matter with the authorities of the country into which he hoped to immigrate. Dealings with foreign agencies, mostly the consulates, to obtain a transit visa or an entry visa were usually as trying as dealings with the bureaucrats of the National Socialist state. In retrospect, the foreign consular officials, who seemed to work at a snail's pace and who often treated the Jewish applicants with coarse impoliteness, showed an indifference that appears disgraceful and shocking when one realizes the situation in which the German Jews found themselves.

Most of the Breesen prisoners were released from the Buchenwald concentration camp on December 6, 1938, as soon as the necessary emigration documents had been procured. They had to sign an obligatory declaration that they had been treated well in the camp and that they would speak to no one about their experiences and leave Germany as fast as possible. The Gestapo did not release Bondy, Scheier, Ernst Cramer, and a younger trainee until a few days later; they returned to Breesen on December 11. For unknown reasons they held two other trainees in the camp longer, the last one until the beginning of January 1939. For everyone the stay in Buchenwald was a severe trial. The fact that most of them withstood it was, in large measure, thanks to their education in Breesen and thus thanks especially to the director of the emigration training farm, Curt Bondy.

The events of November 10 and the succeeding weeks of camp confinement for the older boys, the tormenting uncertainty for those remaining at Gross-Breesen—like the relatives of those carried off to Buchenwald, they did not know until almost the day of release where their friends, sons, or husbands were being detained—proved to be the first step toward dissolution of the training farm. Beyond doubt, the "original" Breesen ended with that day, as Bondy confirmed, looking back a decade later.[46] But there was not only this external break. After the pogrom the Breeseners, like all German Jews, saw themselves conclusively eliminated from the last spheres of life in their native land, in which they had been tolerated until then. This recognition, which followed the shock of the terror they had just lived through, produced among many Jews a reaction commonly known as identity crisis. The Breeseners were not spared this either, as is evident from the few existing records that very clearly express the conflict of emotions in the face of the situation. One of the boys wrote in his diary on the evening of November 10, 1938: ". . . I am a Jew and yet not a Jew, German and yet not a German . . ." And he added the following day: "Truly, one is afraid to be Jewish and ashamed to be German. But one is both and, on the other hand, really neither."[47] With this began, for German Jewry in general and, of course, also for the Gross-Breseners, the painful process of separation from everything that many of them, even after January 30, 1933, had associated with the idea of the homeland.

The pogrom of November 9–10, 1938 had one "positive" result. It triggered an international wave of indignation, and for a limited but precious period of time the borders of a few countries in the world were opened just a bit further for German Jews. This brief opening sufficed to enable the Gross-Breseners of the first and second "generations," thus those who had begun their training before 1938, to emigrate. The majority of the trainees released from Buchenwald found temporary refuge in Holland, in the *Joodse Werkdorp Nieuwesluis* (Jewish Workcamp Nieuwesluis).[48] Twenty-five boys and girls went to England where they could be placed as farmworkers and household help. The Scheiers, Gross-Breesen's physician Dr. Ilse Lehmann, and Bondy himself also went to England. Bondy, though, did not remain there long. After holding a leading position in an English refugee camp (Kitchener Camp) for a short while, he returned to Holland to help as many Jews as possible out of Germany with the aid of the Jewish service organizations there. In the process he directed special attention to the third generation of trainees who had remained at Gross-Breesen, most of whom were in the first year of their training and still very young.

In the summer of 1939 the members of the group who wanted to build their future in Virginia but were still in Germany finally received their entry visas. Four other trainees followed the two training assistants who were already in Kenya, and a group of 21 boys and girls embarked in Rotterdam for Australia.[49] Others went singly to Palestine, the Dutch East Indies, Sweden, France, Argentina, and Belgium. At the end of the year 1939, 118 trainees and 6 former members of the administrative staff were scat-

tered over five continents; thus at least those who had found
refuge in countries overseas escaped Hitler's persecution and extermination measures.[50] But not all the boys and girls of Gross-
Breesen succeeded in avoiding the fate of the "Final Solution."
A small group of those who had been received by the Dutch
Nieuwesluis Workcamp after the imprisonment in Buchenwald
and who did not go to the USA with the Virginia group were
carried off to the Mauthausen concentration camp and killed there
after the invasion of Holland. As will be shown below, almost
the entire third generation of Gross-Breesen perished in Auschwitz.

But once more back to Gross-Breesen.[51] After Bondy, Scheier
(but not Master Kiwi), and almost all the boys and girls of the
first and second generations had left Germany, by mid-1939 at
the latest, the vacant trainee positions were filled. In the summer
of 1939, 114 boys and girls made up the third generation of Gross-
Breeseners. The Reichsvertretung for Jews in Germany, which
was still responsible for the training farm, appointed another educator, Walter Bernstein, as Bondy's successor. In place of Scheier
came a manager named Dingethal, probably appointed by a state
or party agency, who only made guest appearances after the outbreak of war, since he was drafted into the armed forces. He
seems to have been stationed so close to the farm that he could,
in fact, continue to attend to his duties, at least as a matter of
form. It is still unclear who took over his daily tasks. In any
case, Dingethal seems to have carried out his responsibilities
properly and even benevolently, so that the trainees not only received a good education but were also treated decently.

As time passed, the number of pupils decreased. Some, such
as Klaus Freund, succeeded in emigrating. Most of them were
assigned singly or in small groups to the agricultural workforce
on neighboring farms or in forest workcamps, so that in August
1941 the number of boys and girls in Gross-Breesen had declined
to 43. Of the original teaching staff only Master Kiwi remained.
Probably because of an employment advertisement, the parents
of Arthur Wolff, who was already living in Gross-Breesen, came
to the farm at the beginning of 1941, and Arthur's father Walter,
who soon won the confidence of the manager (*Inspektor*), became agricultural director (*Leiter*). Thus the stay in Gross-Bree-

sen was still at least bearable for the few who continued their training there, although after the end of November 1938 for them the training farm was no longer the largely peaceful, sheltered island in the midst of the waves of persecution breaking around them.

On August 31, 1941 the Gross-Breesen project met its official end. The Jewish emigration training camp was closed by order of the Gestapo and its personnel deployed for forced labor (*Arbeitseinsatz*) as an agricultural workforce.[52] That does not mean that all the Jewish youths living and being trained there were immediately taken away, but the dissolution was approaching. In October 1941 the director of the training farm, Bernstein, was dismissed from his position and sent off to a forest workcamp. From there he was later "deported" to Auschwitz, where he died in 1943. In December 1941 Dingethal was replaced as manager by a Mr. Hildebrandt, a party member, who made life difficult for the boys and girls still remaining in Gross-Breesen. He introduced work on Sundays, decreased the food rations, and tormented the young people as much as he could.

Added to that was the fact that as a result of the war the general situation of the civilian population continually worsened, and the Gross-Breeseners were not exempted. Yet even the meager clothing and food allotments that Hildebrandt administered for the personnel were partially withheld from the Jewish agricultural workers—for they were no longer trainees. How much they were afflicted by hunger is shown by a boy's journal that has been preserved. Terse, very objective remarks about the insufficient food rations appear again and again, such as in three consecutive entries in mid-January 1943: "The manor house is declared off limits for us. We have petitioned Hildebrandt about the food." The next day: "Special roll call for all people: 'You have complained about the food, that the food has deteriorated. That's absolutely outrageous. . . . From now on you'll get only what's coming to you. . . .'" And three days later: "So far, no more soup in the morning, no more warm suppers, so that we have to secure provisions on our own. Cottage cheese has also been eliminated. The weekly ration amounts to 125 grams fat and 175 grams jam."[53]

From the beginning of 1943 the manor house of Gross-Breesen was used as a military hospital.[54] So when the renovation work and other preparations began in October 1942, the boys and girls who had been living in this building until then (but also "Aryans" like Manager Hildebrandt) had to move into apartments that had been vacated by the regular farmworkers, where they lived in extremely narrow quarters.

Until this juncture the 43 young people of the third generation still hoped that they could stay on in Gross-Breesen. Cut off from the external world, they nonetheless heard that Jews were being "evacuated"; but they do not appear to have understood what this actually meant. Their greatest worry was having to leave Gross-Breesen and do forced labor somewhere among strangers. "We had an uneventful New Year. We all hope to be able to stay here for a long time yet," noted the young journal-writer on January 1, 1943, about two months before he was deported.

The fear of expulsion from the former training farm was only too well justified. On October 23, 1942 Gestapo officials had appeared and informed the boys and girls that on October 31 the five remaining married couples, all the girls, and six boys, 22 persons in all, would be transferred from Gross-Breesen into the agricultural labor force. Arthur Wolff belonged to this group. They were taken to Grüssau near Landeshut in Silesia, where they were quartered in the famous monastery there. Grüssau presumably served as a collecting center, since many Jews were already there. The group soon lost contact with Gross-Breesen; individual members were deported on different transports. Most of them were probably taken directly to Auschwitz; a few, among them all three Wolffs, were first transported to Theresienstadt and from there to Auschwitz.

Thus 25 boys remained in Gross-Breesen, where they worked through the winter. It slowly became clear to them that they also would have to leave the farm sooner or later, that foreign workers from the East (*Ostarbeiter*) would replace them. The first Russian woman arrived on November 25, 1942, and in February 1943 a group of 40 more Russians followed. Therewith the path was clear to remove the remaining 25 boys from Breesen at the end of February or the beginning of March 1943—the exact date is not certain. Only one of them, Hans Hirsch, survived the genocide.

Thus ended the Gross-Breesen training farm, almost exactly six years after its founding. With it ended the attempt to implant a feeling of personal worth and emotional integrity in a small number of young Jewish people during a time of state-sanctioned degradation and repression, an attempt also to prepare them not only professionally, but also psychologically and morally, for emigration overseas. A considerable number of the trainees as well as Curt Bondy himself came from the youth movement, from which they brought with them to Gross-Breesen not only their nicknames but also their attitudes and views. The Bondy education with its high moral demands gave them additional values and attitudes, with the result that many of them developed a pronounced, occasionally almost arrogant-seeming elitist consciousness. All this constituted the "Breesen spirit" with which they approached all their assigned tasks and which also emerges again and again from the documents in the next chapter.

In this respect, but only in this precise respect, did the Gross-Breesen group have special characteristics; for that reason the group is not representative of German Jewry as such. On the other hand, the experiences of this community mirror in a microcosm the period that was so fateful for all German Jews. Thus several boys and girls from Gross-Breesen became victims in the expulsion of Polish Jews in October 1938. For many others as well as for the Gross-Breeseners, the period of months after Crystal Night, when the often desperate search for emigration possibilities began, was a time of disappointment, despair, and crushed dreams; but it was also a time to think in different ways, to begin anew. It was quite right, wrote Curt Bondy to his former student "Töpper," "that it makes no sense to mourn the *old* Gross-Breesen." There would be new Gross-Breesens "in Argentina, in Virginia, in Australia, in Kenya, maybe also in Paraná . . .; is that not enough for a life's work, and do we have reason to be sad and lose hope?" (document 24).

At least for the first and second generations of Breeseners, who were fortunate enough to be able to emigrate, there actually was no reason to be discouraged. What they took with them from Germany and what no laws and no orders could take away from them were the communal bonds and the character stamp resulting from a short but intensive period of education that was to be decisive for them for decades to come. They also took with them a rootedness in the German cultural tradition that in the end not even Hitler was able to call into question. What they left behind was human beings who were estranged from them, who had deprived their Jewish fellow-citizens of the right to continue to feel like Germans and to live in Germany. So they, who like hundreds of other German Jews had become strangers in their own land, emigrated to other countries, where once again they were strangers for years before they really felt that their new homeland was their home. The search for this safe harbor from a stormy sea demanded not only patience, inner strength, and persistence; it also demanded maturity. The generation that had hardly put away their toys in 1933 matured quickly. Circumstances forced them to bear the cares and duties of adults; on their shoulders rested the responsibility for their own survival and that of others, and they had to prove themselves equal to it. Thus a whole generation missed an important stage of development: their youth.

Before the Whirlwind Hit:
Pictorial Mementos

These snapshots were collected by the author over the past 51 years. They were taken by various people—the boys and girls at Gross-Breesen liked to take pictures. The one of the "Third Generation" with Günther Marcuse on it he obtained as late as 1986. The snapshots reveal for the most part moments of relaxation and play, though a few were taken at work. In the course of moving about during emigration and wartime, the author lost many personal belongings but not his photo albums, some of them by now beat-up old treasure troves that contain pictures taken at a time when the Breesen trainees, like their peers throughout Germany, lived between fear and hope.

The manor house where the Breesen trainees lived. On the enclosed veranda, left, Bondy conducted his weekly "Knowing Life" sessions (Lebenskunden).

Morning formation for daily work assignment.

The endless (and thankless) job of mending the boys' soc

Fifteen minutes of music every weekday evening. Attendance was voluntary. On Sunday nights, with one hour of music, attendance was required.

Unloading fodder.

*Weekend soccer game. The building in the background housed
the carpenter shop.*

*Inside the Hannioten
room. Twelve of them
were living there.*

*Curt Bondy, Gross-Breesen's
director until early 1939.*

"Meui" (left) and "Töpper" in Amsterdam.

Five Hannioten relax on a weekend.

Boys from the "Third Generation" in December 1940. The boy at the far right is Günther Marcuse.

3. The Gross-Breesen Documents

THE FOLLOWING documents, which pertain to the period November 1938 to February 1943, have come into my possession over the course of several decades. They focus upon two central, closely related issues. First was the often frustrating search for a country overseas that would admit young Jews with agricultural training as immigrants. Second was the immediate crisis of the November pogrom facing German Jewry, which made the need for speedy emigration more urgent than before. The fact that these and related issues are commented upon predominantly by young people who were directly affected by the events they witnessed distinguishes this documentation from memoirs and other accounts written many years later, with the benefit of hindsight. It is the immediacy permeating the diary entries and letters that conveys to the reader some of the often near-desperate atmosphere of that crisis period. Few such personal accounts for this phase of German-Jewish history have survived the Nazi years.

That the letters and diary entries were jotted down by still rather young persons is immediately apparent from the style. Thus "Töpper," who came to Gross-Breesen at the beginning, in May 1936, and who stayed there until he left Germany in the fall of 1937, was 18 years old in November 1938, as was his friend "Meui." The latter had once visited Gross-Breesen briefly, and had subsequently emigrated with his parents to Amsterdam, where he attended high school. He spoke Dutch fluently. The two boys, who knew each other from the Jewish youth movement, where they had received their nicknames, met up again in Amsterdam as refugees.

The Töpper documents begin with the efforts made by Töpper and Meui, after news of the pogrom in Germany had reached them, to obtain rather modest funds from Jewish service organizations in the United States. For money was needed to facilitate the release of their Breesen friends from Buchenwald concentration camp, where, as I have related, they had been imprisoned in the wake of the pogrom. At the time release from camp could be speeded up if proof was submitted to the Gestapo that those imprisoned had been granted permission to enter another country. In the case of the Gross-Breeseners, the destination in question was the refugee camp Nieuwesluis Workcamp (Werkdorp Nieuwesluis), an agricultural transit and training facility in Wieringen, North Holland, that the Dutch had established for young Jewish emigrants from Germany.[1] And permission for the Breesen group to come to the camp hinged on outside financial support, which would have to come from somewhere. Meui's and Töpper's liaison man in New York, Joseph Loewensberg, was the brother of a Gross-Breesen training assistant, Ernst L., who with three trainees had emigrated on an individual basis and was then living and working at Hyde Farmlands in Virginia. Joseph had visited his brother at Gross-Breesen before the latter emigrated, and for this reason was well acquainted with the whole project. More important, he had close contacts with several Jewish refugee service organizations in New York.

The concluding document, the diary entries of Günther Marcuse, was not part of the original German edition owing to space restrictions arising from the general format of the series in which the book appeared. Günther Marcuse came to Gross-Breesen on February 18, 1939, after his parents and sister had emigrated. He thus became a member of the so-called third generation of Gross-Breesen trainees. He stayed in Gross-Breesen until the end of February or early March 1943—his last entry in the diary is dated February 26—when he was deported to Auschwitz, together with the few remaining Breesen trainees, and perished there in March 1944. Thus, Günther spent four full years at Gross-Breesen, longer than most of the other trainees. However, as the farm ceased to be an emigration training center after August 31, 1941, when the Gestapo turned Gross-Breesen into a labor camp, Günther and his friends became for all practical purposes slave workers who were treated as such by the farm manager. The diary starts on October 6, 1942 when the remaining Jewish trainees were ordered to move into new quarters because the manor house, where they had stayed until then, was being transformed into an army hospital. What exactly prompted Günther to start a diary at this particular juncture one can only surmise. Presumably, he sensed that everything was closing in on him and his peers, and he wanted to leave a record behind. This was not unusual at the time—one need only recall the Ringelblum Diaries from the Warsaw Ghetto. The exact way in which the diary survived is not completely clear. According to the account of another Breesen trainee who survived, Günther entrusted the diary to one of the wounded soldiers who was treated at Gross-Breesen military hospital, and gave him the address of his family in England with a request to get it and some other personal papers to the family once the war was over. This was done, and the original of the diaries, together with letters and some personal documents, was deposited by Günther's sister, who now lives in Israel, at Yad Vashem Archive in 1969. A translation of the diary was first published in 1970 by Professor Joseph Walk, Jerusalem, in volume 8 of the *Yad Vashem Studies on the European Jewish Catastrophe and Resistance*. Professor Walk also wrote an introduction to the diary. I have used part of the translation, have reformulated a few passages in a somewhat different way, but am basing most of the information given here about Günther Marcuse on the pioneering work done by Professor Walk.

Günther Marcuse's diary is a very moving document. As he was born in September 1923, he was a little over 19 years old when he made his first diary entry, and thus only a year older than Töpper was when he commented on the November pogrom in the fall of 1938. But the two diaries differ in form and tone. Whereas Töpper's observations tend to be rather lengthy and often emotional, Günther's are terse and matter-of-fact. And yet, between the lines of his entries, which combine remarks on prosaic

matters with comments—barely veiled—on the ever-tightening
noose, his mounting apprehension emerges about a future over
which he had no control whatsoever.

To keep this edition of the documents within acceptable limits,
a selection from the letters and diaries was necessary, and some
documents had to be shortened. In Günther Marcuse's diary, some
entries were eliminated and others condensed because they would
be of little or no interest to the reader (e.g., comments on specific details of the day's work in the fields). In the other documents, primarily private matters, technical details, and repeti-
tions were omitted. All such omissions are marked by ellipses.
Throughout the documentation, I have made every effort not to
impose any censorship but to abide strictly by the selection cri-
teria just mentioned. My primary concern has been to provide
as undistorted a picture as possible of the prevailing conditions
and the problems that grew out of them. Except for the Marcuse
diary, which is at Yad Vashem in Jerusalem, all the documentary
material on which this study is based is in the archive of the
Forschungsstelle für die Geschichte des Nationalsozialismus in
Hamburg.

Finally, a few words on the identity of the persons who are
for the most part mentioned only by their first names or nicknames. Some of the former Gross-Breesen trainees with whom
I consulted before the publication of the German edition requested anonymity. To comply with their wishes and, presumably, the wishes of others not consulted, surnames are given only
if they appear innocuously in the documents. They are in most,
although not in all, cases the names of individuals who were
adults at the time, and very few of them are still alive today.

1. FROM TÖPPER'S DIARY

AMSTERDAM
November 10, 1938

Why has it been so long since I made any entries? I don't
know! . . . The last months and weeks were grim and stren-

uous, in both big ways and small. In September we nearly had a major war, and the world was in a flurry of excitement and tension. [The emigration project] USA is still in the works, and one must wait, wait, wait. October 30 was the first anniversary of my leaving [Germany]. A quiet, fateful day for me. [. . .] All this pertains to my small personal life, my trifling self. But how insignificant it is compared to the big events. In September, Germany annexed part of Czechoslovakia and there was nearly a war. [Divided] Europe faced each other in arms, ready to get at each other. Was it all a bluff? Who knows?! In any case, the statesmen of England, Germany, Italy, and France concluded a so-called peace, swore to deal faithfully with one another, but in fact used and still use it [the "peace"] merely as a breathing spell for further rearmament. But Germany has now become powerful, a factor everyone in Europe has henceforth to reckon with. All countries are afraid of that dictator who has made so much out of nothing; and their fears are justified.

The day before yesterday, on November 8, a young Polish Jew made an attempt on the life of the German Legation Secretary in Paris, von [sic] Rath, who died yesterday as a result of his injuries. This assassination, essentially a mere act of revenge— blind and thoughtless—was prompted by last week's deportation from Germany of thousands of Polish Jews, who had been deprived of their Polish citizenship.[2] For this reason, Germany threw them out just a short while before [the Polish measure took effect]. Today, Germany replied to the assassination with a "pogrom" that is being carried out quite systematically. The synagogues in Berlin are burning, Jewish stores have been looted and ransacked, and Jews are being arrested and face a terrifying and uncertain fate. In the course of this week, more laws are to be passed as the state plans to proceed against the Jews [officially]. The German people have had it. They've degenerated, are messed up, are being systematically corrupted by plebeians who call themselves leaders. The situation of the Jews is dismal. There is hardly a country left that still lets anybody in; there is hardly a state in which the term "anti-Semitism" does not exist. And yet, it [life] will go on. All will have to grit their teeth and endure. How cowardly I feel, sitting here, abroad, writing these things. How much I would rather be in Germany now, with my friends. Who knows what's happening to them? I won't be able to write to them until tomorrow.

Awful, this feeling of prostration. Why are we so helpless, why is there no more justice in the world? Is there a God? [. . .] Strange, I am a Jew and yet not a Jew, a German and yet not a German. I believe in God, but then, I don't really believe in him. And that's how it is with everything. Halfness, that's us; halfway we dwell, are only halfway guests, halfway we live, I live. But I want to be a complete entity, must find my way, must get out of Europe, go somewhere where there are only a few people, but lots of animals, forests, mountains, a secluded world. [. . .]

Perhaps New Breesen will materialize sometime. Then I shall have a mission again, different from helping out in my father's store. But all this is again "I," and what matters now is exclusively that group of people in Germany whose religious faith has turned into a Damoclean sword for them; people to whom I belong, but who in the last analysis are not my people after all. Yet regardless of how matters stand, who and how many of them I acknowledge, I want to and must help them as best I can. Ablaze, like beacons of hatred, destruction, and senselessness, the burning synagogues in Germany flare toward Heaven which either does not exist or will remain silent until the Obersalzberg,[3] too, turns into a sea of flames—the Obersalzberg, and along with it a regime of death and terror.

AMSTERDAM
November 11, 1938

I feel very down. The terror in Berlin and in Germany goes on. One dreads terrible "laws." Nobody knows what's going to happen. [. . .] "A hitherto unprecedented stain on Germany's history," write the Dutch newspapers. Indeed, one is afraid to be Jewish and ashamed to be German. But one is both and, on the other hand, is really neither. Crazy, crazy, crazy. The worst is that one can't do anything, that one must watch helplessly as people dear to one are dispossessed, mistreated, and perhaps even killed or imprisoned. Meui, with whom I spoke briefly, is in the same state as I. [. . .] Otherwise there is nothing more to be said.

AMSTERDAM
November 12, 1938

In the evening, Sala called and told me that he has read in *Het Volk* that Bo [Bondy] and twenty GBers [Gross-Breeseners] have been arrested.[4] I've checked; it's true. I can't write anymore to-night. Tomorrow we must try to find out how we can help! [. . .] I am determined *never* to forget this. I want to help, want to try everything to do something about it. And sometime I'll take re-venge, for this must not go unpunished. Bo arrested! I want to help, I must help!

---

2. TELEGRAM (COPY) TÖPPER AND MEUI, AMSTERDAM, TO JOSEPH (JOE) LOEWENSBERG, NEW YORK

November 13, 1938

NEWSPAPER REPORTS ARREST BO WITH 20 BOYS / SPEED UP WASHINGTON[5] / LETTER FOLLOWS / TÖPPER

---

3. TÖPPER TO JOSEPH LOEWENSBERG

November 13, 1938
Dear Josef!
This letter is not only for you, and I ask you to pass it on: to Hyde-Park Farm [*sic*], to Thalheimer,[6] to Dackel's brother if he should be over there, and to Borchardt.[7]
What is happening in Germany now you most probably know in part from the press and the radio. Terror is sweeping through Germany such as has never happened before. I have met an ac-

quaintance here who succeeded in fleeing [from Germany] and who is altogether unable to report coherently. Yesterday Sala called me in the evening and told me that he read in the Dutch newspaper *Het Volk,* one of the three big papers here, that Bondy and twenty boys were arrested. I shall quote the relevant passage for you: *Het Volk,* November 12, evening edition. Translated from the Dutch. "Near Breslau, at a training facility for Jews who want to earn their living abroad as farmers, the Gestapo staged a raid. The director, Professor Bondy, and 20 trainees were arrested. One boy, 17 years old, was told: "Grünspan, the murderer, was only 17 years old, and that's why we are arresting you in particular!'"

Furthermore, I received today an express card from four Breeseners who just that day [of the raid] happened to be in Berlin and who write me that they are all right *for now,* but that in G.B. all people over 18, including Bo and Scheier, were arrested. Of course, they did not write this openly, the way I do now, but it was so clear that I wonder how the card got through.

I have sent you the telegram, Josef, so that the Wash[ington] letter[8] will be issued, as it is due, anyway. Once we have this piece of paper, and it must be possible to get it, then the best thing to do would be for Borchardt and Thalheimer to get in touch with some lawyers and try and get the people out through this approach. It's a slim possibility, but perhaps it will work. We must try everything, everything to help a little. Every person who can be gotten out of that hell over there must get out. We cannot help everybody, but if everyone tries to do his utmost, then it must succeed, at least to some extent. We are abroad and thus must try everything. Look, I don't have to write to you what it means to be arrested. It may last for 3 hours, it may last 30 years. It can merely mean detention, but it may also mean K.Z. [German initials for concentration camp], and therewith torture and death. Lord, it's all so unbelievably awful! Let's suppose, the boys and Bo and Scheier should be released; then every day they had to spend inside [Germany] would be agony.

Our Jewish youth has become rather weak, and we all know the state the young generation is in. But does this mean that the remainder, those who are still relatively strong, who still have opportunities to achieve something, are going to be broken as well? Those who until now have stood up to everything, the youth, are being systematically crushed and will go to the dogs unless help comes soon, somehow. We cannot restore their former vigor to the older generation even if a part of them should succeed in getting out, but perhaps we can still save the boys and girls, can get out people whose energy is still intact!

I myself am powerless. I can only write and pass on to you what I hear from over there [Germany]. All of you, Heinz Kellermann,[9] Haka, all those who care about the people over there, you must commit yourselves with all you have. And not only in regard to the Washington letter, for unfortunately, it can only help get a few people out, if it should be issued in time. But try to find people with enough initiative and connections to help effectively. Try to find people who will give affidavits. Try to find influential people who can appeal to the [U.S.] government. Drum into the people there [in the USA] that up to now America has always been a land of rescue and freedom, and mostly for people who were not as much in need of assistance as the Jews, and especially the Jewish youth in Germany [today]. Shouldn't it suffice, on a continent like North America, if one handed a newspaper to an American today and said: "Look, this is happening to people who are no different from you, you, you? Their only crime is that they are Jews. America is big, and although there are unemployed, the Jews will help to create new jobs in your country; and what do half a million people really amount to if one drags them literally out of hell? Is America going to collapse as a result of it? No! Will the drawbacks be so awful? No!"

Look, must any more be said? I believe that the boys now at Hyde-Park Farmlands [sic] don't feel any differently from the way I feel when they imagine how people they are close to are now being hauled about somewhere in Germany, with their fate less than certain; boys whom one knew for the most part as well as oneself, not to mention Bo and Scheier. And I believe that we can help them. Once the requisite papers are there, one can have them released from detention, and then get them out of Germany, too.[10] And even though we are dealing at the moment

with only a small group of people, that would be some help. Try
to persuade those who gave affidavits to renew them, as I am
in doubt about the whereabouts of the original ones. They lay
in Bo's desk, and only those given by relatives have been submitted [to the U.S. Consulate in Berlin]. They were to lie there
until the [issuance of] the Wash[ington] letter. Perhaps they could
be sent directly to the consulate, together with the [Washington]
letter, but the people in charge of it will surely know how to
handle this. The main thing is that something be done from the
[U.S.] government's side. I have spoken only about the Breesen
[boys] for the most part because their fate is very, very important
to me. I don't think I need to emphasize this. And I repeat that
if one helps those who, in my opinion, can be helped, one is
doing quite a lot. But there still remains the [collective] fate of
the others, which is neither better nor worse; for them one should
also try to find a way out.

Whether and to what extent this will be possible, nobody can
say, of course. But the Breesen [boys] can be helped, and I hope
that you'll succeed. I shall list the names of those who presumably have been arrested and who are known to you, at least in
part; it is only a fraction [of the total number arrested]: Bondy,
Scheier, Dackel, Juwa, Knirps, Prinz, Manfred, Klaus Herrmann, Ernst Cramer, Klobü, and all the remaining boys over 18.
As you probably know, they were a large component of the trainees. Those named here are presumably along [with the arrestees]
because they were in Breesen that day. Jochen and Leus, Traut
and Stef are still in Berlin for the moment, and we must fear for
them as well. If the example of Frankfurt am Main should set
the pattern (the arrest of all Jewish males 18 to 60), then we
must also be afraid for these people now in Berlin.

I don't want to write any more now. This letter may be somewhat chaotic, but it should be comprehensible in spite of it. I'm
waiting especially for news from you, Josef! Although I have
not written exclusively to you, please don't be angry about this.
[. . .]

Try to get results, okay? I'm waiting to hear from you shortly.
Give my regards to all I know.

Best regards to you. . . .

4. FROM TÖPPER'S DIARY

November 13, 1938

Mostly correspondence. One letter to Josef Löwensberg for help, then one to Leus' uncle in London so that he may possibly let Leus come to him. In the forenoon we sent a cable to New York that Bo and twenty people have been arrested and that they should hurry up the Was[hington] letter. In the afternoon Fritz Bondy[11] came, and I briefed him about events. We also spent the evening with him and cabled a second time that they should do something for Bo in particular and, above all, to include him in the Was[hington] letter. The evening with Bo[ndy]s at some family's in Beethovenstraat was completely dominated by the impact of events. Everybody knew somebody who was or still is in detention. The newspapers report awful things, and the letters from over there [. . .] speak volumes. But something must, will have to be done. Went to bed at 2 A.M.

AMSTERDAM
November 14, 1938

Meui has contacted Dr. Elk from the Wieringen Committee[12] to explore the possibility of getting the Virginia people admitted [to Nieuwesluis Workcamp]. We submitted our request in writing and still hope to get a reply this week. Since all this must be financed (we're dealing with approximately ten people), we cabled to New York for $300.00 until [their] departure [from Holland]. Let us hope! Letter from Leus, but no other news.

AMSTERDAM
November 15, 1938

There is suddenly a possibility for requesting [admission into Holland for] immediate relatives. [Fritz] Bondy has submitted a request for his brother. The committee advised us by all means to submit requests for all those arrested [. . .]. We telegraphed to Breesen in order to obtain precise personal data and wrote a letter to the committee in which we requested entry [permits] for those arrested. Holland wants to establish two refugee camps, limited to 10,000 people. That would offer opportunities. I am dead tired and shall go to bed. Where are the Breeseners sleeping now? How are they faring? One must sleep and help, not brood.

5. TELEGRAM (COPY) JOSEPH LOEWENSBERG TO TÖPPER

November 15, 1938

BECAUSE OF UNCLEAR SITUATION OFFICES HERE UNDERTAKE NOTHING NOW REGARDING VIRGINIA BOYS / LETTER OF CREDIT LEFT FOR AM- STERDAM / DOING EVERYTHING POSSIBLE FOR BONDY

6. TÖPPER TO JOSEPH LOEWENSBERG

November 16, 1938

Dear Josef!

This is the second letter to you, although the first one has not yet left because this time the mail boat had such poor connec- tions that I decided to wait until the departure of the *Normandie*.

This morning I received your telegram, and you can probably imagine that I was rather downcast. Please do not consider this a personal reproach. I know very well that you, Heinz Keller- mann, and now probably Hilde Meirowitz,[13] too, are doing everything you can, and I assume that certainly the gentlemen at the committee, i.e., Mr. Borchardt and Mr. Thalhimer, are doing their utmost as well. But despite all this I'm writing again, and despite this I shall send a brief separate letter to the National Coord[inating] Committee in order to approach these gentlemen once more directly.

Above all, I want to let you know briefly what we're doing

now from this end. After we sent off the telegrams on Sunday, immediately on Monday we approached the directors of the local Jewish Workcamp "Nieuwe Sluis" in Wieringen. There we put in a request that the boys belonging to the Virginia group be admitted, with the right to work there until they can emigrate, so that they will be released from imprisonment. We don't know where the boys with Bo and Scheier have been carried off to. The workcamp is more than full, and they only promised us that there will be a conference within the next few days at which our case will be discussed, and that everything possible will be done to help these people. Yet they stated as a condition that, first, the people concerned would have to be in possession of affidavits, with the probability that they be granted immigration into the United States soon; and, furthermore, that monthly financial support money for these people would be forthcoming, as a norm approximately 40 guilders a month per person. Now we turned first of all to you in America, via cable, because we ("we" are Meui and I) expected, and still hope, that most of the assistance for the people has to come from you. Since Bo was not included in the list for the Wash[ington] letter we have asked, and ask you again, that if you are successful [with the Washington letter], you also try to enable Bo to come over; and if at all possible, also Scheier, who as an academically trained agronomist would have the best chance at getting a job. Parallel with our efforts on behalf of the Virginia people Dr. Fritz Bondy, Bo's brother, who lives here, has filed an application with the [Dutch] government here to let his brother come to Holland.

On Tuesday, thus yesterday, the newspapers reported that Holland intends to let in approximately 10,000 people and to intern them in two large camps until the nations find a way for the Jews to move on and settle in colonial countries. As of now, though, nothing is definite, as the other countries have not yet made any move; Holland has contacted them by telegraph. But there is a real possibility that a certain limited number of German Jews will be allowed to enter Holland. The local Jewish Committee let it be known last night that immigration requests for immediate family members may be made through the committee, and that this should be done in a hurry. Thereupon we telephoned the committee and, by sheer luck, got through. We described the situation of the arrested Gross-Breesen people and asked for advice. We were asked to list those arrested by name, with as many precise personal data as possible, for the benefit of the committee, and to request that they be permitted to come to Holland. They had heard about the case. Thereupon we wrote to the committee and asked that above all the people not of the Virginia group, including Mr. Scheier, be admitted to Holland, and pointed out that these people had an excellent chance, as trained farmers, to be admitted very soon into a colonial country. We also pointed out that Fritz Bondy had submitted a request [for entry] for his brother. We shall have to wait and see what develops.

Today your cable arrived, and we felt compelled to raise the money here somehow, so that we do not forfeit possible admittance [of those arrested] to Wieringen. Through Meui's connections, via a local lawyer, we got to a Christian church committee, and Meui, who explained the matter to these people, received a qualified promise with a request to do all we can to raise the money somewhere else. That we'll try now once more in the USA. These people here, of course, were already inundated, but they did promise us help in case of emergency. Tomorrow, perhaps, the decision on the Virginia people will be made, and then we shall see what can be done. I forgot to tell you that today we turned also to an old local juvenile judge, a friend of Bo. He is well known here and has connections to the top. He, too, promised that he would give us all possible help he can muster.

Josef, there must be a chance of getting the necessary money together! The local committee asked initially for more than 40 guilders, and in the cable we asked for $300.00. Now that we have the cable from over there [USA] we have arranged for fl.40.00 per person, and in the $300.00 we have figured in that the boys will probably get out without any luggage. Try everything you can to get perhaps even as little as $150.00 a month by way of a guaranteed sum. All this may look as if we were out for money, and we're haggling. But we've concluded that even if one could find over there no more than ten wealthy people willing to send $20.00 each month to Holland, then a small group of boys who intend, and still hope, to get to the USA can be put up here in the meantime, at least temporarily. Don't you think that 20 [*sic*] such people could be found? Josef, conceivably some might consider my letter incredibly cheeky, pushy, impertinent, and sponging; but I believe I won't have to explain, to you fellows over there least of all, that we're not doing this for ourselves, or for me personally, but that we're concerned about people who are in a terrible situation and with whom we wanted to build a new life together and whom we must help, or at least try to, with all means and all effort possible. I know that if it were up to you, who know these people personally, everything would probably be arranged by now. Alas, you, too, are only emigrants and can only entreat and pass on whatever information reaches you. I can well imagine that next to my request [for money] lie hundreds like it on Mr. Borchardt's desk, and that the committees there do not know where they ought to begin to help. And yet, I ask you to do whatever can be done. I do not want to write a letter to the NCC[14] in which I tell them something of what the people, *all* of them and those arrested in particular, are going through over there [in Germany]. It might give the impression that I wanted to arouse pity in order to get results. But aside from the fact that I don't want to do it, I believe that it won't even be necessary.

In America one undoubtedly reads in the newspapers a lot about what's happening, but nobody *sees* the faces, those fearful, hounded faces of the few lucky ones who crossed the frontier illegally and who have *not* been turned back. Where you are, one cannot listen directly to the terrible experiences these people relate, how they were chased through the streets like cattle, how their personal belongings were thrown into the street, how men and *women* were beaten, and how they strayed—and still stray—through the woods near the cities in order to avoid arrest and not fall into the hands of the Gestapo and perhaps be transported by the notorious SS guards to a concentration camp. All this one reads about and gets upset in America, but one does not hear it close up, and you have not yet received those letters from Germany with appeals for help as I, for instance, am getting every day, letters that say nothing—and that say everything. There is fear of being arrested, of hunger, of misery. Fear of what is going to happen, the anxious question about what portends to be a dismal future. Where to go? What to live on? America has been, and is, a free country. Can an American visualize that people must fear for their lives, day after day, week after week, and—this not in wartime—unarmed, unprotected? That boys 18 years old are being arrested and carried off somewhere, boys whose survival is being steadily endangered with every day they spend in the custody of the Third Reich? Isn't it obvious that two generations are systematically being annihilated?

I don't want to and can't go on reiterating any further. The way it is, here we can continue trying to help these people only if we don't keep thinking about what's happening to them, both to the Breeseners and the many thousands of [other] German Jews. We must still give thought to the following: First, if we should get the news that the Breeseners have been released, or some of them are, then there is virtually nothing we can do from here anymore and we must rely exclusively on the Washington letter. And even if it should come, it is only a partial solution. GB, in my estimation, can no longer go on functioning, for who will be able to pay even a cent? As a training farm Gross-Breesen has up to now cost money; it had been taken over with a deficit but could continue to operate because of outside contributions. By now this has become virtually impossible, for the Reichsvertretung will be unable to contribute any longer, and the fathers of the training assistants and trainees are [now] utterly poor, and moreover, most have been arrested. The future existence of Gross-Breesen is probably a matter of weeks as far as this can be gauged right now. At the moment it is being run exclusively by Mrs. Scheier, whom I admire and respect like virtually nobody else. And yet, all this is only provisional, and the question now is what is to be done? [. . .]

Second, we must weigh the possibility that Wieringen might refuse [to admit] the Virginia boys. To put it briefly, there, too, I would see the Washington letter as the only solution. The backup project Kenya that Bo had begun to tackle shortly before the pogrom is a Nothing as it has, in my view, not the slightest chance. [. . .][15] Josef, this has been a difficult letter for me.

Look, I know how you and Ernst and Haka and Rolf worry about your parents and relatives, and I know that you, too, can only do for your parents, for Breesen, for Bo and Scheier what is humanly possible. Please forgive the mistakes and corrections. It is now one-thirty in the morning, and as a result there are some unclear passages and typos.

T.

7. FROM TÖPPER'S DIARY

AMSTERDAM
November 16, 1938

In the morning a cable came from New York with a refusal. However, a little later today Meui obtained a promise from a local Christian organization that they would jump into the breach if that became necessary. After lunch we visited a Dutch friend of Bo, Juvenile Judge de Jongh,[16] quite an old but rather a well-known man. He promised us every possible assistance he can render and wants to write to the ministry on behalf of Bo and the boys. In the afternoon the chances for immigration into Holland already looked less positive. Well, one must keep on hoping and not lose one's head. In the evening we wrote to the NCC, New York, and I wrote until 2 A.M. to Joseph Löwensberg.

AMSTERDAM
November 17, 1938

In the morning came a telegram from New York in which they assured us that everything possible would be done. I went to [my father's] store where I found a message from Meui to the effect that Wieringen has given its consent. We went to the committee and filled out the requisite forms. Then we put in a call, charges reversed, to Stroppen [near Gross Breesen][17] in order to get the names of the arrested Virginia boys and of the others who were also arrested. I talked to Ruth Hadra and Mrs. Scheier but was unable to elicit any reply but "Leus will write to you." We put in a call to T's in Berlin, and Leus answered the phone. I put my questions, but she did not give an answer either, at least none that was useful. I asked her to send a list. To the names of Prinz, Dackel, Knirps, Gert Fränkel, Klaus Herrman, Kiwi we added Juwa's name, as he has a chance to obtain a Brazilian visa. In the evening, additional letters to the NCC, Josef Lo[ewensberg] and the committee. I hope we'll succeed!! We cabled replies to New York.

8. TELEGRAM (COPY) TÖPPER TO JOSEPH LOEWENSBERG

November 17, 1938

BESIDES BOSCHEIER [BONDY AND SCHEIER] 20 ARRESTED, OF THOSE AP-
PROXIMATELY 8 VIRGINIA BOYS / WERKDORF OVERCROWDED / AT MOST
8 PLACES PROMISED FOR AFFIDAVIT BOYS / SEND FINANCIAL AID

9. JOSEPH LOEWENSBERG TO TÖPPER

November 17, 1938

Dear Töpper,

Finally I'm getting around to writing you a few lines, shortly before the departure of the *Queen Mary*, and acknowledging your three cables [as well as] my two cables. I would like to bring up just a few facts and, in doing so, try to separate the wheat from the chaff; otherwise I could write you for hours and for pages.

After receiving your first cable together with Fritz B[ondy's], which I found when I came home late Sunday evening, I got everything moving immediately. Right away on Monday morn-

ing I sent a cable to Th[alhimer] in Richmond and also informed
Ingrid Warburg[18] here. Then later I found out that Th[alhimer]
is here [New York] at the moment, and that was good. Then
Monday evening I received your [second] cable that another 20
boys had also been arrested, and I passed it on at once by telephone to Ingrid W. and Thalhimer at his hotel, as well as to
Heinz [Kellermann]. It's quite terrible that we are so powerless
in the face of all these things. Then Ingrid's father was also arrested in Hamburg, and on Tuesday morning came your cable
asking whether $300 could be raised, which I immediately passed
on to the appropriate authorities, which I had gotten in contact
with in the meantime. On Tuesday morning I had had breakfast
with Th[alhimer] [at] 8:15 A.M., and Tuesday noon Heinz and
I were also at the council [National Council of Jewish Women]
for two hours, where Ingrid has her office. Then in the evening
the first night cable went out to you, and we sent you another
one yesterday evening, to which I expect an answer tomorrow
morning. Of course the $300, and even more if necessary, can
be raised, but at the moment the people don't want to do anything in this matter but keep trying [to get results] via Washington. That means in plain language: the Washington letter that
you mentioned several times in your telegrams isn't even there
yet. Let's hope that it will be possible to get things in line from
there.

    This evening, Thursday, there was an announcement that Ger-
many is not letting anyone out at all until the penalty of one
billion is paid, and it is believed here that the boys from the
training camps have been sent to do fortification work on the
western border. But nobody knows anything that's specific or
reliable because we aren't hearing anything from Germany itself.
Where are you getting all your news from? Were there some
contacts with people in Germany? How do they plan to get the
10 people out? Presumably by sending them to the Workcamp
at Wieringer Sea (*Werkdorf am Wieringer Meer*)? By the time
you get this letter we will probably have exchanged a few telegrams and these things will be out of date, and I suppose, too,
that some of these questions have already been clarified in your

letter to me. You can imagine that the people here at the [National Coordinating] Committee want to do something, especially for the Breeseners, but they don't see how, at the moment, and hope that Washington will now do something about this case. It must be hard at the moment, too, to find the people, since they can't still be in Breesen, in any case.

In Bondy's case it was clear from the beginning that he can't come on an affidavit; instead, he has to get an appointment as a professor, and by *presenting this employment contract* he can come here outside the quota *immediately*. On Monday/Tuesday/Wednesday there was nothing to be done, and yesterday Thalhimer went to Richmond again, and today he let the offices here know that Bo will receive an employment contract from Richmond, so that he can come outside the quota. Do you have any idea where he is and how he can be gotten hold of when this employment contract is ready, which will be the case in just a few days? Today I haven't spoken to Ingrid myself, because I couldn't leave the office, since I've frequently been absent for hours at a time the last few days. But Heinz brought this good news from Ingrid. Please inform Fritz Bo[ndy].

I'm writing this letter in a big hurry, you'll notice, but it certainly has shown you that your efforts are meeting with a response among us here. All the best.

Yours,
Joseph

10. TELEGRAM (COPY) JOSEPH LOEWENSBERG TO TÖPPER

November 18, 1938

MONEY AVAILABLE IN CASE SPEEDY RELEASE POSSIBLE THROUGH YOU / REQUEST SCHEIERANG [SCHEIER AND] NON-VIRGINIA-PEOPLE FIRST / WE KEEP TRYING RE BONDANG [BONDY AND] VIRGINIA-PEOPLE / KEEP US INFORMED

11. FROM TÖPPER'S DIARY

AMSTERDAM

November 21, 1938

In the morning first at the committee, then to the Children's Committee because of children's transport.[19] Meui spoke with Mrs. van Tijn, but she won't have a meeting with the relevant people until tonight, when she will also bring up our problem concerning "all" the Breeseners. [. . .][20] In the afternoon to the store [father's] and in the evening briefly at Meui's, then home, read, went to bed. Idiot that I am I have chosen at this point to read Feuchtwanger's *Geschwister Oppenheim*,[21] a novel about a German-Jewish family. Everything the heart desires is treated here: concentration camp, torture, the works. Where might our boys and Bo be now? We must prevail. And to do so I need strength. And strength I'll get through hatred, and that in turn through the thought about this . . . [unreadable word] of the past two weeks. Do I still love Germany? Yes, three times yes, but differently, in a more qualified way than before. A lot of people will have to be put up against the wall before a *Reich* can be created again that commands respect. Today I read a beautiful verse, though I don't know by whom:

> *And loveth thou Germany?*
> *The question is absurd.*
> *How can I love*
> *What I am myself?*

Yes, I can, namely that Germany which is within myself. And that will have to last as a substitute for a long, long time. But it will do.

AMSTERDAM

November 22, 1938

Nothing important except a letter from Pong's mother who asks me to do something for Pong, who has been arrested. At the same time Vici asks me to get him out [of Germany]. But it won't work! I may barely manage to get the other people [from Breesen] out, perhaps not at all. And then there is always that combination of fear and hope on the part of the people over there [in Germany]! At night came a letter from Mrs. Scheier's sister requesting news.

November 23, 1938

In the morning to the committee. After a wait of three hours it's my turn. Before de Jongh talks to van den Bergh[22] they can't do a thing. Boiling, I go to Meui. We telephone de Jongh who said, rather sadly, that he had spoken [with van den Bergh?] and would so much like to help; but unless he is given specifics he cannot do anything. I give my bicycle to Meui, and he rides to the committee to see Mrs. van Tijn. Meanwhile van den Bergh had telephoned Mrs. van Tijn, and Meui is greeted with the news that all boys will be admitted and that notification, or rather the dispatch of [entry] permits, depends only on getting an address [to where permits should go]. We call Leus in Berlin, who asks that all mail be sent to her address. She is very composed. When I arrive at the committee with this information they want a different address. As they are about to go home, we reach an agreement that I shall come by again tomorrow. In the evening still briefly with Meui. Then early to bed.

---

12. TÖPPER TO JOSEPH LOEWENSBERG

November 25, 1938
Dear Josef,
[. . .] We contacted the local committees at once and, with luck and connections, reached the people who count [and] from whom we received yesterday the assurance, after lengthy palavers back and forth, that all boys will be claimed, and that they will be granted temporary residence in Holland. What happens

then will depend for the most part on America (especially as far as the Virginia boys are concerned), and in part on the ICA[23] in Paris (for the ICA group), and in part (for the remainder and, if anything should go wrong with the other projects, also for the two aforementioned groups) on the solution to the colonial question as far as it affects refugees. But alas, we aren't that far yet. We are also afraid that the boys may have been dragged off to the western border [of Germany]. Bo, according to our information, or rather that received by Fritz Bondy, is in the concentration camp Sachsenhausen, near Berlin. A cousin of Fritz B[ondy]'s, who arrived here with a visa for America the day after we sent the latest telegram off to you, had met a man in Berlin who was with Bo.[24] More we do not know. —Yesterday came a telegram about Bo's employment contract [in the USA], but we didn't know then who sent it. Now it's clear to me, and it would be just dandy if this would work out.

[. . .] All boys on the list have been arrested and are to be claimed from here; this was not an easy task, as Holland lets in only those people who have been approved by the requisite ministry, except for [those going to] the special training facility at Wieringen. Special, by the way, is the wrong word. What I mean is that it is enough if one receives an entry permit from Wieringen, for this means that one will be interned in Wieringen, so to speak, and may not live anywhere else until one leaves the country. Now Wieringen already has too many trainees, and there is literally no barrack available yet for the boys. Apparently they plan to put up additional accommodations to provide at least provisional quarters. The places [for the boys] have been promised to us, and all future moves now depend on Germany.

[. . .] Every day Meui and I receive letters in which we are asked for help. And we haven't even managed to get those people out who fall under the category of "extreme danger" (*Lebensgefahr*). All we can do with the others is to counsel patience and to try our utmost to get out first all those who have been arrested, although I know how awful it is for all the others, too, those who don't sleep a single night at home but are always on the run, even now, afraid of being arrested.

[. . .] I'm checking through your letter once more to [make

sure that I] reply to your questions. You ask where my information comes from about what's happening in Germany. Here,
so close to Germany, one knows much more, of course, than in
America. Daily Dutch nationals are coming from Germany who
give reports and tell things. Jews who had a valid visa for another country in their pockets came here helter-skelter during
those horrible days, and up to now I haven't talked to a single
one yet who didn't leave everything behind in shambles. I receive regularly camouflaged reports from Berlin about G.B.
[Gross-Breesen] and Berlin. [. . .] Whatever one hears is just
awful, beyond imagination. This is not Germany anymore but a
country of cannibals who no longer deserve to be called human
beings (*Menschen*). According to refugee reports, a large portion
of the [German] population is deeply outraged; but there were
still enough around to deprive 600,000 people more or less of
their livelihoods and homes.[25] There is no use at all, however,
in dwelling on this. We simply must try to help, and help again.
I hope that we'll accomplish something. [. . .]

---

13. JOSEPH LOEWENSBERG TO TÖPPER

November 25, 1938

[. . .] I would like to single out from your letter the three
most essential points that are undecided at the moment, and answer them.

1. Deliberations are pending with Washington authorities
that seem not unfavorable for the Virginia boys, and as it looks
today, they promise to be successful. Thus, first of all we
would like to get the non-Virginia boys out of Germany by
all means, since something is being done from Washington,
we hope, for the Virginia boys. Non-Virginia boys include
Scheier.

2. Regarding Bondy, Richmond University has prepared a

contract for him, and if everything works out, he will get out under non-quota on the basis of this contract, which will be possible very quickly, that is, immediately, when he has been found. That will be the next problem, but in view of the co-operation we hope to get from the American authorities in Berlin, a solution for this will be found, too.

3. You understood us correctly: We are prepared, that is, the committee is definitely prepared to give the required $300, and beyond that will also sponsor more agricultural people within certain reasonable limits, up to 50 people, who can be gotten out of Germany and later brought over here. [. . .]

---

14. FROM TÖPPER'S DIARY

AMSTERDAM
November 26, 1938

[. . .] In the morning at the store, in the evening at Meui's. [. . .] In between Frosch was here, from Wieringen, and told me that he has heard via G[ross] B[reesen] that Schnauzi, Isi, [and] Inge Salomon have been deported as Poles.[26] Didn't go to bed late.

AMSTERDAM
November 27, 1938

After I spent some more time with Frosch I found Hilla waiting for me when I got home. [. . .] She told me that Breesen has been smashed to bits. The SS stole money, typewriters, etc. It is awful. The boys seem to be in [concentration camp] Buchenwald. I just phoned Schwarzschild,[27] who confirmed the receipt of the border crossing passes for Prinz, Juwa, and Paul Hirsch. The boys must get out very, very soon. Hilla leaves on Thursday for Australia. [. . .]

AMSTERDAM
December 2, 1938

At noon, mail came from America. Financial aid of any kind pledged, going even beyond the sum required for the boys for whom we have put in requests. The Wash[ington] letter looks favorable; Haka even writes about an immediate positive decision. I replied at once, and in between received a telegram from Schwarzschild to call him [in Berlin]. We telephoned in the evening. The release of the boys has been ordered, but it may still take another day or two. Kenya has accepted the great majority of applicants, and America also looks favorable. [But] one cannot say anything definite yet. I am so far neither [on the list] for America nor for Kenya [as a prospective immigrant]. Crazy, but I won't panic. First the boys must get out, and then we'll see what happens. [. . .] Time will provide an answer. We must wait again. But the boys and Bo will probably soon be free. Let's hope.

AMSTERDAM
December 3, 1938

Heard nothing from Berlin. In the morning and afternoon at the store. For no special reason I was very down and depressed. [. . .]

AMSTERDAM
December 4, 1938

[. . .] A day of rest and no positive news!

AMSTERDAM
December 5, 1938

I am very sad, don't know why myself. No mail from Berlin. In the evening St. Nicholas gift giving. We all exchanged presents. [. . .] Otherwise nothing. I am waiting, waiting, waiting. . . .

AMSTERDAM
December 6, 1938

Fantastic! In the morning came a telegram to the effect that all boys, except for Bo and Scheier and four more, have been released. I wrote immediately to them and to Schwarzschild. Lord, I wish they were here already. In the evening mail came from Schwarzschild, Jochen, and Stef. [. . .]

---

15. TELEGRAM CURT BONDY, BRESLAU. TO DR. DAVID WARMBRUNN,[28] AMSTERDAM

December 11, 1938

EVERYONE RETURNED HEALTHY FROM TRIP PLEASE INFORM MY BROTHER IMMEDIATELY / CURT [BONDY]

---

16. TÖPPER TO CURT BONDY

December 11, 1938

Dear Herr Bo!

It's great after such a long time to address you in this way once again. This morning your brother phoned and told us that you had returned, and you can well imagine how glad I am.

I assume that you're now facing a number of rather harsh facts. Everything has been turned completely upside down during the past four weeks; everything is quite different from what it was until the day you stepped out of the course of events. Plans have been scratched, new ones have taken their place, old ones have become more acute but have changed shape. Despite all this I believe that you will find your way very soon again in these new

circumstances. Very much will depend on you, probably more
than you may be aware of where you are right now. Of G.B.
[Gross-Breesen], although it is still operative, all that remains of
it in practice are its nimbus and its past.

Thus, please do not take offense and don't consider it impertinent or presumptuous on my part if I, your student, tell you
today that your place is now out here. From here, with the support of the committee and a number of rather influential private
persons, you can contribute a lot to the emigration of the young
from Germany. When I say "here" I mean both here, Holland,
and also America. We expect in the very near future your temporary residence permit [for a stay] here in Holland, which would
also have some personal significance for you. For when you know
that after you accept that call of yours to [a college in] America
you can still spend some time here in Holland, then you'll probably leave [Germany] somewhat easier. That permit we expect
any day now. We owe this opportunity largely to the cooperation
of Meester de Jongh, who has gone all out for you in a mar-
velous way, both for you and for the boys. I hope that everything
will soon work out. In addition, your name and that of Gross-
Breesen have had a lot of impact, as both enjoy here a thoroughly good reputation. [. . .]

Herr Bo, there's so tremendously much I could say. Those
many oppressive, cataclysmic, stormy events that have occurred
during the past weeks may well have changed and marked us
all, most of all those of you in there [Germany]. Although now
it may look at first glance as if fate has torn us apart, scattered
us far and wide, I still believe, despite everything, that neither
you nor the boys have been broken, and that the ring which has
kept us together to now has not snapped. Impossible to say at
the moment what the future may bring. There will probably be
upsets, separations, difficult times. You may have to watch some
of your life's work go down the drain. And yet I believe that
what will remain with you will be the certainty that you have
not labored in vain during the past months and years. To be sure,
some of the things that seemed meaningful to us and to our objectives will be ruined, but whatever was inherently valuable cannot

be destroyed; it will remain. Behind us and you lie the beauty as well as the weight of the past years and weeks. But something also lies ahead of us. Neither your life nor ours, with tasks and experiences ahead, is over. It will be much harder, will look differently from what we had envisioned originally. But there it is, a road we must take even though it's not the best one, like the one we once picked out on the map. Perhaps this road will lead us to the same, our first objective, although the incline may well be steeper, the distance greater. We shall have to see. But the main thing now is to realize that roads still lie ahead of us, something that's extremely fortunate. For how many thousands cannot even see a path anymore?!

In all probability our people will be scattered in the very near future throughout all parts of the world. Even now some of our friends are in North and South America and in Africa. But somehow we could recognize them were we to fly invisibly across the continents in search of the Breeseners. Some common manners and similar characteristic qualities we all have; and these are no superficial, shallow characteristics, as we know very well. And since you probably will have a hard time now giving up your work [i.e., Gross-Breesen], always remember that your true, real work, your work with people, will not stop at all but will go on as something manifold, beautiful, and strong that will go with us over the entire world: Gross-Breesen.
I salute you, Herr Bo!

---

17. TÖPPER TO JOSEPH LOEWENSBERG

December 16, 1938

Dear Josef!

Please don't be angry if I write only briefly today. The sole important thing to report is that six [Breesen] people arrived here in Amsterdam yesterday—Dackel, Juwa, Prinz, Herrmann Kiwi, Floh, and Paul Hirsch—and by now you should have received the telegram pertaining to this event. This first group will go on to Wieringen on Monday, and [the names of] additional boys have been submitted [to the committee] for processing. All boys as well as Bo-Scheier and Kiwi have been released from concentration camp.[29]

Now the following: there are three issues I ask you to take up with the agency over there:

(1) The NCC must immediately contact the local committee here in regard to the financial question. The people here wrote to Mr. Borchardt on November 18 but so far have not received a reply. The sum in question is forty guilders a month per individual.

(2) In an enclosed letter we have asked the NCC for a certain sum—to be determined by the [NCC] people there—to be used for pocket money for the boys. They have crossed the frontier with insignificant amounts of money (10 Marks), and that won't last very long, of course. The boys need pocket money for shoe repairs, barber, etc.

(3) Furthermore, you wrote me at the time that the people there had declared their willingness to provide for up to fifty people here in Holland. We had asked the agency in question, if they agreed to this, to send a detailed telegram to the Dutch government. Now Bo is very much interested in this project, inasmuch as it would open a number of possibilities for the creation of a transit camp here, if it should be approved; but this would require as a prerequisite a written guarantee about the money. Then negotiations would have to continue over here. Thus, please ask the people in charge over there for a clear statement on the matter. [. . .]

18. CURT BONDY, GROSS-BREESEN, TO TÖPPER AND MEUI

December 19, 1938

Dear boys,

Today I received your long letter [not extant] and shortly afterward the gratifying telephone call came that we may send fifteen additional people to Wieringen. For the moment we have made up a list of only eleven people, but in any case request that the four openings be reserved for us. The fact is, we signed up for Denmark some of the people who were on the trip [in Buchenwald]. But the decision about Denmark will not be made until sometime this week.[30] If it should turn out to be negative, which is improbable, then we would sign up more of the Denmark people with you. Is that clear and acceptable? [. . .]

---

19. TÖPPER TO CURT BONDY

December 21, 1938

[. . .] Early today I was at the committee and [. . .] there submitted a list [of further Breeseners], asking to reserve four additional places. Thereupon he [?] said to me: "Listen here [. . .], up to now we have just asked for personal data, nothing else. All this means nothing yet." Needless to say, I said nothing further but asked him when I should come back. He told me to come next week. Thus, I must ask you by all means not to accept either the list or the possible admission [of the Breesen applicants] as fact yet. What I want to tell you is that I am certainly counting on permission for the boys to come here to be granted. But as we've had setbacks before, I'd rather be a little more cautious than overly hasty. [. . .]

---

20. CURT BONDY TO GERTRUDE VAN TIJN

December 24, 1938

Dear Mrs. Van Tijn,

I have received news of my boys who have now arrived in Wieringen, and I honestly owe you and your colleagues my heartfelt thanks for all that you have done and continue to do for us.

With great joy and deep gratitude I learned after my trip of the different emigration possibilities for the Gross-Bresseners, and above all, the chance to stay in Holland during the waiting period. It was especially pleasing to us that the boys could continue to learn their profession and have good accommodations during this time. We sincerely hope that the boys' stay in Wieringen won't last long and that they can soon get to their destinations.

A group of them are to go to Hyde Farmlands, the farm put at our disposal near Richmond, Virginia. The preparatory work (light and water installation, etc.) is in full progress. Five boys are already at the farm, and the latest news from the USA gives us reason to hope that the immigration problems that still persist will be cleared up in the near future. My recent visit to the American Consulate General in Berlin proved to me that the project is being pursued with serious interest here.

Among the boys who are being proposed now are a number who are to go to Australia. This project is similar to the one in Virginia in that about thirty boys and girls are to be sent to [a] [. . .] farm, and we hope that our agronomist [Scheier] and his wife, who have been in this work for many years, will become the administrators there. The last cable from Sydney was quite positive, and the permits are expected soon.[31]

So we hope that this group, too—if you give them permission to come to Wieringen—will occupy their places there only for a short time.

It might interest you to know that five other boys of ours are going to Kenya. It is expected that they will spend a short period of time this year yet in England. So fortunately we will not have to burden you with them.

We are trying to bring about emigration as fast as possible for as many as possible, especially for the older Gross-Breeseners, and we have reason for hoping to accommodate some of them in Denmark as a temporary solution.

If changes have occurred occasionally in our proposal lists, it is because a small number of our people haven't yet returned [i.e., from Buchenwald], for others sudden emigration possibilities arise, and the list of those going to Denmark is not yet quite settled. And finally, sudden emigration possibilities are sometimes found for the parents, who then take their children with them, or hopes of emigration turn out to be unfounded. So please don't be angry when changes occur now and then in our proposals.

According to the news we have received, we can suggest five more people who could *perhaps* be sent to Wieringen. We request that you wait a few more days on this matter, until we have certain news about the accommodations in Denmark.[32]

In expressing to you once again my heartfelt thanks for your admirable work, with kind regards, I am

Yours faithfully,
[handwritten] Bo.

21. TÖPPER TO CURT BONDY

December 29, 1938

Dear Herr Bo!

In the past, whenever the year came to an end, we all tended to wish one another a "Happy New Year." One got drunk, sometimes more, sometimes less, made all sorts of wishes for the coming year, and [. . .] succumbed completely to the spirit of New Year's Eve. —When I got to the age when I began to live consciously, this began to change. At year's end we usually stood in the snow, high up in the mountains of Sudetenland, and then skied with flaming torches into the New Year—wild and impulsive, to be sure—and yet silently; and for the most part, we even reflected on what we were doing. And then came the end of the year at GB [Gross-Breesen]. In fact, I happened never to be there on the day itself; but I wrote letters, and in that manner experienced a new way of "celebrating" New Year's Eve: to put it somewhat tritely, we took stock of the past year.

I still remember that last year I wished you happy success for all our plans. At that time, everything was extremely uncertain for all of us. Projects hovered in the air, were discarded, then resumed new life again. The people in Breesen began to rotate;

familiar faces disappeared, new ones showed up. But Breesen
remained. Somehow we anticipated the New Year full of ex-
pectation. We all knew that it would not be an easy one. We
braced ourselves for disappointments, but on the other hand, were
not without hope. And then came the year 1938 with its tem-
pests. I shall not enumerate the individual stages that lay between New Year's Eve 1938 and New Year's Eve 1939. It has
been a long and trying struggle, a year of waiting, a year of
disappointed and again rekindled hopes, a year when life was
tumultuous and rough. —For you personally the year ended with
a blow. You sowed Virginia—and reaped Buchenwald. And both
are more than names, more than a destination or an experience.
They are symbols. And the latter symbol proved the stronger.
What one year of hard work failed to accomplish was achieved
within four weeks. All Breeseners now see a road ahead, and
yet, at the bottom of our hearts we are not happy, not genuinely
happy about it. Something firm was torn asunder, something solid
broken. Of the Hannioten,[33] some will go to Virginia, some to
Kenya, a third contingent to Brazil, a fourth to Argentina. And
that's how it is with everything, that's the way with Breesen,
that's the way with all the Jews in Germany. If we want to draw
the bottom line for the year 1938, we must admit that all the
plans we had seen in an idealistic light have collapsed. On one
level there will be settlements, will be a Virginia [project], and
Breesen will continue to operate. But for those of us who see
and expect not expedients alone, more fell apart on November
10, 1938 than just externals.

And yet, we must not mourn now. I know that you're not
doing so; you know that I would often like to do so. But the
year has also been an object lesson, a cruel one, to be sure, but
an object lesson nevertheless. We have learned what a human
life is worth, how unimportant is the fate of an individual in the
last analysis. We must not mourn, and under no circumstances
grieve for what's gone and done with.

Before us looms lots of work, on a large scale for you, on a
small scale for myself, [and there are] new obligations, objectives. Our G[ross]-B[reesen] is gone, died quite suddenly, just

like Stella died, or Hannio, or Gustl.[34] It seemed senseless and cruel to us. But even here life confronted us again with sober fact, and it was and will be up to us to build from the debris a new springboard for the future. In a short time from now, Breesen will be to all of us merely something we carry within ourselves and which, one hopes, will mark us outwardly, too. But this is quite a lot, and whoever was truly in Breesen will take away more than most others.

We have learned not to make any more plans at the end of the year. It is actually one of the worst symptoms of events that we, including myself out here, have become more indifferent and somewhat fatalistic. Actually it should be our task to welcome in the New Year in exactly the same active spirit [we displayed] when we skied down the white mountain slopes with torches. In that way we wanted to express an attitude: let's go forward and charge unconditionally toward the new, the unknown, or a new duty . . . [or] a new task. This time we shall not, nay, do not want to ask ourselves, half scared, half hopeful: "Shall we spend next year in Virginia, in Kenya, or in Brazil?" As far as I am concerned, I'm determined not to ask such a question, and I believe that quite a number of us feel the same way. We have recognized the senselessness of making plans, have seen how everything built up during years of work was swept away overnight. I am now facing the future. I do not want to anticipate everything but shall try to find a place that I, too, can fill and where I can work. And that will be, as far as it is possible, with Breeseners. I want to be given the chance to build up again, to commit myself to something that's meaningful. I shall write you soon about the technical aspects separately, but I would like very much to go somewhere where I can work with you and a segment of our people.

Yes, we have indeed been dispersed! Jochen, Stef, Dackel, Prinz, Töpper—soon everyone will go somewhere else. And you yourself don't yet know what you should do and where you want to go. And although it would be crazy and shortsighted to delude ourselves as to the extent of such separations, it is my opinion that precisely among these people, precisely among you and the

Hannioten, that last bond that has held us together will not be severed. I do not want to say any more about this because it is difficult to talk about it. But I believe that you, too, will feel the same [. . .] once this letter reaches you and you are walking through the rooms where we have experienced so much together and, above all, where we have *lived*.

The year 1939 begins with a question mark, and everybody goes into it more or less with a sense of "Lord, can anything worse happen to me? I don't really care anymore." For this reason I want to ask you today to convey New Year's greetings to the few people who [still] know me and to tell them that the old saying "everything changes" still holds meaning for us, too; that life lies ahead of us, waiting for us, and ready to provide everyone of us with tasks and duties, happy and serious times, the way it has always been since man was created.

For you personally I have actually wished and said a lot already in this letter. Please forgive me for always using the plural form. I had no intention of placing myself on an identical level with you. Whenever I wrote "we" I meant all those in whose name I thought I was speaking, although they do not—and probably never will—know the content of this letter. And you are one of those who are part of them. That's why this [letter] may have sounded to you a little weird at times. There's lots I could write to you yet tonight. I want to thank you for so very much that the past year has brought. I can express it only in this provisional manner. I also want to thank you for the book that you sent along with Dackel. If I want to wish something for the New Year, then it will be, as mentioned earlier, to be reunited with you during the coming year, to build up something together, and to do some meaningful work again.

Herr Bo, last year we hoped for a year of accomplishments. This time I can really wish us only courage and hope; let that be the spirit in which to enter the New Year. We'll be just as unable as last year to control events, but we can do again what we did then: to endure in the manner and attitude suited to us whatever may come our way, and to try and make the best of it, regardless of what happens. At New Year's I shall be again with the boys up there [in the Nieuwesluis Workcamp], and then we'll think of Breesen. Herr Bo, I give you my hand and send you my cordial regards.

---

22. TÖPPER TO JOSEPH LOEWENSBERG

December 30, 1938

Dear Josef!

Unfortunately I missed the mail boat last time, with all the bustle around here, and I ask you not to be angry with me over this. You cannot possibly imagine how wonderful it was after such a long time to have Breesen boys here again. It is simply not possible in this cramped space to tell all that happened to them. They did not relate much, especially in the beginning, after they arrived. But their looks conveyed more than anything else did. Aside from their shaved heads, two of the boys, Prinz and Juwa, were [physically] not in any shape to move on and had to stay for a few days here [in Amsterdam] before going on to Wieringen. But during the first four days [after arrival] all of them stayed here and gradually recovered a little.

Buchenwald had been depicted by the local [Dutch] press as the most infamous concentration camp, and rightly so. The boys have told me that they realized how much less the life of a human being was worth than that of an animal, and that one could be simply beaten to death if one said or did anything, however insignificant, that the SS did not like. When Bo left the camp (he was the last one, together with Scheier and two boys), the camp physician there said that in the course of four weeks, 400 people had died. —I don't want to write more about it right now. You know, it is useless to keep visualizing all this over and over again, because one merely gets upset once more, and that doesn't help. I believe that once we can enter the "Land of the Free," soon, I hope, the boys will be able to tell you about life in a German KZ [concentration camp] with greater detachment.

At the moment we're glad above all that they're out and safe. At first they were unable to grasp it at all. The nightmare of that regime is unbelievably powerful, and when the boys here in Amsterdam crossed the street diagonally, for instance, rather than straight, they still visualized a man rushing up to them, yelling "Jew." [. . .] Now at least they are out in Wieringen, and tomorrow, on New Year's Eve, I shall go out there again. I was also there at Christmas and have taken a look at how and where they live. They're staying in a barrack with a bedroom and dining space and have already started working. It is so overcrowded out there that when I visited for one night, I had to sleep in a table turned upside down, with a mattress placed inside. But now 370 acres of additional land have been bought, and chances are that the workcamp will be enlarged. Unfortunately, nothing is official yet, but it is very probable.

[. . .] Schorsch is still in Buchenwald because he was not registered as a Breesener when he was arrested and thus was excluded from the [successful] efforts undertaken by the director of Winkel [training farm], Gerson, to free all those imprisoned.[35] I believe I've written you about this. It is wonderful that even in this day and age there are still people around who do not lose their heads and who have indeed accomplished the improbable. Schwarzschild, too, has worked like a madman.

This has been the more personal part of my letter. Now I must write you about some of the technical aspects, and want to answer your questions. Altogether, 21 boys are to come to Wieringen. Up to now only 8 have been definitely admitted, 6 of whom are already there. Negotiations continue about the remaining 13. It is a question of the Virginia boys and the Australia boys. You may have heard, perhaps, that while the boys were in the [concentration] camp, Schwarzschild made every effort to take care of them [in regard to emigration]. Thus there emerged, besides Virginia, also the Kenya project and the Australia project. The first one has already shown some success. The boys in the Kenya group—Jochen Feingold, Ernst Cramer, Mösch Braun, Heinz Lichtenstein, and another one whose name escapes me at the moment—will be going to England in the course of this week, and probably early in January on to Mombasa. Australia is planned for 30 boys and the Scheiers, so that preference was given above all to those who up to now have had no concrete final destination for emigration. That things got shifted around in the process was probably inevitable. Some of the Virginia boys grabbed at Kenya,

and in turn Bo has added some others to Virginia. Negotiations
are taking place about all these [projects] with the agencies concerned over there. [. . .]³⁶

As to emigration into the USA, negotiations are taking place
in Berlin right now that seem to be going not unfavorably. Bo
has real hopes now of seeing us move on [to USA] soon. May
his wish enter the consul's ear! But I almost assume that you
will be better informed on this matter than I am. —I had asked
in my last letter to you and the committee [in New York] for
some pocket money for the boys. Meanwhile the boys have learned
that they will receive [at Wieringen] 50 cents [Dutch] a week,
so that there is no longer any need [for pocket money from the
USA]. Please be good enough to pass this on. The boys, of course,
want to make as little trouble as possible, nor do they want to
make demands—that's understood. By the way, as soon as they
can find the time and the necessary peace of mind, they will
write themselves to the agencies over there.

[. . .] You are wrong in assuming that I have relinquished
my [U.S. emigration] quota number. As soon as one applies one
gets a number automatically. It's not as extreme as in Germany
where one receives numbers up to 20,000, but the crush is nevertheless real, so that everybody gets registered and, depending on
the state of his application, is given a quota number. Subsequently, when he wants to enter [the United States], this [num-
ber] fixes exactly the place and date where and when the visa
will be issued. Now when the pogrom wave started to sweep
through Germany, the local consul here took away the assigned
numbers from all those who in his opinion were not emergency
cases and put them at the disposal of the consulate in Berlin, or
Hamburg, or Stuttgart, in order to enable people whose application for immigration [into the USA] had been approved in
principle, but who had a number with a long waiting time, to
get in with the lower number from the consulate here. I have not
even been personally notified of this, but it became common
knowledge; and when I asked a lawyer here who specializes in
[emigration to] North America, he confirmed it. An acquaint-
ance of mine, however, who had been asked earlier to come on
December 21 for a physical examination [to the U.S. consulate],

did receive a written cancellation because he had a definite appointment. He was told that he would have to wait one, two, or three years longer. That just my number would be spared under these circumstances was highly unlikely. [. . .]

Bo is trying in Berlin to get as many Breeseners as possible out [of Germany] without delay. He also negotiates with the consulate in his own behalf. That's all for today that's worth telling. [. . .]

---

23. CURT BONDY TO DR. OTTO HIRSCH[37]

December 30, 1938
On the way from Berlin to Gross-Breesen

Dear Mr. Hirsch,

You surely have many and important things to do, but I would nevertheless like to appeal to you by letter, as it will perhaps be necessary for you to make decisions about my case there [on a visit to London].

Now, as ever, what I said to you in our last conversation applies, [i.e.] that I am willing (provided I am permitted) to stay on in Germany if I am given a really important task to carry out. Since I only have to look out for myself, I can dedicate my further efforts to areas in our rescue work in which I can be used most importantly and effectively.

I only want to stay in *Gross-Breesen* until most of the people are out. This is even more important now that Schwarzschild, who worked incredibly hard and successfully for us, is emigrating in the next few days. So are Martin Sobotker and Alfred Hirschberg.[38] I will be quite superfluous in the continuing administration of Gross-Breesen once the people presently there are essentially gone. This is all the more true, as Gerson has already found an agronomist who is willing and would surely be capable of overseeing Gross-Breesen. Gross-Breesen will have to give up its present character, in any case. I no longer believe that we will be allowed to create the sort of institutions for which you would want my assistance.

The question remains whether there are other important pedagogical or organizational tasks here in Germany for which I, especially, am needed. If not, then I would be free for assignments outside Germany. Hyde Farmlands doesn't need me at the moment, as Seligsohn wrote.[39] However, I could very probably go to Richmond as a professor with a non-quota visa without any trouble.

The next question is whether it isn't more important, to begin with, that I work in Europe and not in the USA. That brings up again the plan that Schwarzschild suggested during our last discussion and that we talked over with Hannah Karminski once again today.[40] This is how it looks now:

First I would go to Holland for a few months, or, if that isn't possible, then to England. My tasks would be approximately: Assistance in

1. Creating more possibilities of placement for children and youths (up to 25 years old) in European countries (individual and group accommodations, partly as a temporary solution).

2. Taking care of those placed in these countries.

3. Taking charge of further emigration to other countries.

In addition, it should be said:

1. A serious petition for a residence permit in Holland has been filed for me.

2. My position can't be a private one; rather, I would have to be a special delegate of the Reichsvertretung of the Jews in Germany.

3. Since I will probably emigrate with 10 Reichsmarks, my living expenses, travel, and other costs will have to be provided from someplace. I don't want to have more money than I absolutely need.

From there you will be able to judge the necessity and possibility of such work better than I can here. I have repeatedly heard the view here that not nearly enough is being done, above all for non-Zionist youth, that should and could be done.

I would be grateful for a speedy reply, even if very short.

I wish you successful work there.

With kind regards,
Your

24. CURT BONDY TO TÖPPER

January 1, 1939

Dear Töpper,

Recently many letters have come from old Gross-Breeseners, and all of them express the genuine bond with Gross-Breesen. More and more, and with real joy, we are learning how many of you have taken action for our cause in recent weeks and are trying to help us. The number of letters from people who were here in the past and who want to be able to work and live with their old friends again sometime and someplace is amazing.

Unfortunately we can't write thorough individual answers to the many letters we are now receiving. Your letter, however, raises some fundamental questions that I would like to answer fully.

I understand well that some of us are getting tired and are losing hope, but I believe that we mustn't do that and that we, of all people, unquestioningly have a responsibility to dedicate all our energy to an attempt at a systematic reconstruction. You write: "If we want to draw the bottom line for the year 1938, we must admit that all the plans we had seen in an idealistic light have collapsed." Exactly the opposite is true. All the plans that we are pursuing now are no emergency solutions; rather, they belong to the overall scheme that we drew up in the past year. Of course, long ago we gave up our first plan that all Gross-Breeseners would live together on one single farm; and I don't think we should be sad about that at all. On the occasion of his farewell, Ernst Cramer told us very clearly that his view of Gross-Breesen when he came here was wrong. Gross-Breesen couldn't be a narrow circle of friends in which everything the people from the youth movement had imagined as ideal was realized. But Gross-Breesen, he said, was a circle of really good comrades who agree on their professional goals and their human behavior. Then and now, and actually to a greater degree than earlier, the Gross-Breeseners have a very particular mission to fulfill. This applies to their careers as farmers and to their conduct and to their type of communal life. Whether our new settlements succeed in becoming a model and extending their influence depends on us. Therefore the new Gross-Breeseners have very definite and far-reaching responsibilities to carry out.

You write, "in a short time from now Breesen will be to all of us merely something we carry within ourselves and which, one hopes, will mark us outwardly, too. But this is quite a lot, and whoever was truly in Breesen will take away more than most others." I think that is absolutely right and there is no sense in mourning for the *old* Gross-Breesen now.

Look, that would be the same as if people leaving their youth were to mourn continually for that time, as if their values were irretrievably lost. People who understand how to live know very well that when they grow up, the experiences of their youth represent an important and essential component of their existence as adults. That's the way it is with Gross-Breesen, too. Gross-Breesen near Obernigk is preparation and a time of youth; the Gross-Breesens in Argentina, in Virginia, in Australia, in Kenya, and perhaps also in Paraná should represent real and good adult life and confirmation of it. My friend, isn't that enough for a life's goal, do we have any reason to be sad and lose hope? Maybe all our plans won't be realized, yet our duty is basically determined and we are not here to wait and despair; rather, we are, especially right now, obliged to carry out rather significant tasks. It is no fantasizing to imagine that in the next few years we will build up new settlements in different countries, and we know that in some places very energetic and effective beginnings have been made. [. . .]

Now you have to admit that the comment in your letter: "We have learned not to make any more plans at the end of the year," really isn't right. But it will depend essentially on ourselves whether more or fewer of these plans are realized in the new year.

And to close: you yourself have no reason at all to complain about lack of plans and of courage. We know very well how much you have worked and accomplished for Gross-Breesen just recently.

So: the new year will be full of important, good, and fulfilling tasks for us Gross-Breeseners.

Affectionately,
Your Bo

---

25. CURT BONDY TO HAKA

HYDE FARMLANDS, VIRGINIA, U.S.A.
January 11, 1939

Dear Haka,

I just arrived from Berlin. You have surely heard about our telegram to Thalhimer today. [. . .]

In England, matters developed in such a way that a possibility turned up of settling people in agriculturally needy areas. We had despaired that anything would come of the Virginia project, and decided to approach the consul. In the morning Friedel took a letter there from me in which I requested an appointment, and I actually got one on the same day at three o'clock. After a short discussion, the consul said he would be willing to give us agricultural preference quotas and immediately filled out forms with the annotation "agricultural preference."[41]

He set as conditions:

1. an individual affidavit for each applicant with the necessary data
2. a certificate from the farm (probably from Thalhimer) that
    a. the applicants would go to the farm immediately, and
    b. own a share of the farm.

This declaration must be made for each one individually, and I hope that when this letter arrives the certificates will already be on their way. [. . .]

In addition, the consul said he would be willing to send a copy of the correspondence with the [State] Department to the consulate in Havana (one person), in Warsaw (two people), and in Rotterdam (five people).[42] I assume that now with this there will be no more difficulties, nor for the others either, in getting on the preference quota list. I even presume that the matter will go relatively quickly, since the consul told me that we should send in the papers as soon as a person has completed them, so that they can be processed immediately.

You can imagine how very happy we are about this solution. [. . .]

---

26. TÖPPER TO CURT BONDY

January 13, 1939

[. . .] Now I don't know again where to start. Being an egotist, [let me start] with the new, apparently rather positive-looking America project. First of all I have the following question: What does the term "preference" mean in this particular context? It can mean immediately, but it also can mean two more years, considering that others may still face five more years [of waiting for a visa], and then, compared with these, it would indeed be "preference." But I really believe and hope that in this case we are dealing with something that will now definitely materialize?! I'm now waiting above all for your letter so that we can see what will have to be done. [. . .]

---

27. CURT BONDY, GROSS-BREESEN, TO FRITZ SCHWARZSCHILD, BERLIN

January 20, 1939

Dear Schwarzschild,

Last night I got back from Berlin and would like to report to you briefly on the status of our projects.

1. *England* (interim emigration 300 people—so-called herd list) to which the ICA people as well as the Australia people had applied: fell through; apparently committee disputes. Whether the matter will get going again is questionable.

2. *Children's Transports.* As far as our people are concerned, the matter has fallen through. Except G.S., who has a private financial guarantee, surely no Gross-Breesener will be able to leave.

3. *Denmark.* Have heard nothing further. Must have also fallen through.

4. *Virginia.* Is continuing well. People just received numbers for the preference quota. Today Dackel wrote that he was at the Consulate in Rotterdam with Töpper. The consul was acquainted with the matter, nice, held out the prospect to the people that they would be able to leave in March. [. . .]

5. *Transit camp.*[43] You have probably already heard the details from the newspapers there. I am enclosing a circular from the RV [Reichsvertretung] for your information. As Günter explained it to me, all sorts of problems over who is in charge have arisen. [. . .]

Whether or not I get my passport will be decided tomorrow. I have been summoned to Breslau.

6. *Gross-Breesen.* Difficulties on account of the farm-workers' *(Inst)* apartments. We are now making enlargements and repairs on almost all apartments; they will be completed in four weeks. Costs, 2,000 to 3,000 Reichsmarks.

My successor: A school teacher, Bernstein, and wife are prospects. Capable people. For Scheier: an Aryan manager *(Inspektor)*, still uncertain.[44]

So, that's all the news to report, and I hope you are completely back in the picture again.

Sincerely yours

---

28. TÖPPER TO CURT BONDY

January 20, 1939

Dear Herr Bo!

Many thanks for your letter of the 17th, or 18th, as the case may be, of January. The result of the trip to Rotterdam came as quite a surprise. I had expected less. Special appointment numbers [*Vormerknummern*] don't exist in Holland, at least no special forms. 16 persons a month are assigned preference status, and as the quota for February was already filled, we have been placed on the March quota. Now the following is important: The local consul seems to assume that he will receive all additional documents and papers, as in the past, through the American consul general in Berlin, and only then will he notify us about the physical examination. As soon as the requisite documents reach you in Berlin, I would suggest that these be passed on, with the pertinent comments, to the consul in Berlin, so that he in turn can send them to the consul here [in Rotterdam]. If the consul in Berlin is satisfied with the papers of the remaining people and passes on ours, I'm confident that the consul here will not be difficult and will summon us. I'm also not yet clear whether my affidavit will have to be renewed again. It would be important for me that it be resubmitted by the original sponsor as he is, of course, known to the consul by now, and besides it [the affidavit] would be more than enough in this case. He [the sponsor] is the director of one of New York's largest banks. I shall ask Josef [Loewensberg] once more about it, for on the basis of past experiences I could well imagine that people might conceivably say: "Oh, well, he has already applied and the affidavit is being processed, so why contact that man once again? Everything will be all right!" —But I am convinced *that* it will have to be renewed because I applied in July and was turned down.

The matter of the boat tickets for the boys is very unclear to me. In my opinion it will not be possible for the parents to pay for them! That was still possible a short time ago, but I believe only for [tickets to] South America. Would you mind contacting the committee on this matter? I also believe that all German boats are booked full until June; in this case it should prove more advantageous for one of the two committees to pay for the crossing than to pay for the more or less fruitless stay here. Of course, I exclude myself from all this! [. . .]

Herr Bo, it is so mortifying that we always have to rely on the charity of others, of strangers. We who in the past were even embarrassed when somebody merely gave us an invitation are now forced to rely on the aid of all kinds of wealthy, unfamiliar people, some of whom may, on the one hand, want to help very much indeed, but who at the same time expect in return commitments and a certain demeanor toward them that I find exceedingly detestable. I believe that all of us will do our utmost to get into a more independent situation as soon as possible. Sometimes I feel like an animal that eats out of somebody's hand, but not like a dog, which does so gladly, but rather like a trapped wild animal that knows exactly: if I were not trapped I would not eat anything. —But this is our fate, and we must now try to pay our debts as soon as possible and to become independent of other people's aid. But about that more when we talk; soon, I hope.

I like the boys a lot, at least most of them. Prinz has hardly changed at all, though he looks ahead more clearly now and gives a lot of thought to what he wants to do with his life. Too bad that he won't come with us. But that's looking at it from a personal angle, and I can well imagine that Prinz especially may do better if he has to rely only on himself. [. . .][45]

Y. is, or rather is on the way to becoming, the type of financier only concerned about himself, somebody who will ruthlessly stop at nothing when it concerns his wallet. When he's in a good mood he can be decidedly nice and pleasant; but woe to anybody who might ask him for a favor when he's in a bad mood. Then he turns mean, the way his forefathers probably were when they were still doing business in the vicinity of Lvov and Yaroczin, peddling suspenders. I am sorry to have to judge him so harshly, but I believe that I am right. [. . .]

I'm getting on well with Dackel and the Hannioten in general, but best with Prinz and Dackel. We were just now together in Amsterdam and Rotterdam for two days, and it was great. He [Dackel] is undoubtedly pigheaded and always tries to get his way, but this, after all, is not a shortcoming. He runs the group rather well, although some friction here and there is unavoidable. More or less all concerned are at fault. He has not changed much, though he has become a little more manly since I saw him last. [. . .]

Herrmann, after being rather dejected and downcast during the first days here, is now the same as before. Often, when the mood up there at the camp [Nieuwesluis] is depressed, he pulls them out of it with his sense of humor and his natural manner. He's the one who helps Dackel most, and who is best suited to do so; for aside from being rather clever, he also has a good deal of influence on the people and, besides, possesses the necessary calmness to be persuasive. But he wasn't really back in his element until the moment when he had a saw in his hand once again and wore a carpenter's apron. Whereas during the first few days the spirit of the mother prevailed, that weak and low-spirited woman, it is now again the drive and the energetic manner of the father that are coming through.

Floh is as he always was. Unchanged, [he is] in part still the big baby, in part the boy who knows exactly what he wants and is going after it most resolutely. Whenever it's his turn to make sure that everything is orderly [in the barrack], I am reminded, with a deep sense of horror, of certain Sunday mornings.[46] Whatever is not neatly in its place is thrown onto the individual beds, accompanied by invectives in Karlsruhe dialect, and woe to those who do not put their things away. The two non-Breeseners in particular can tell you a thing or two about that (in my opinion they have ample cause for lamentation. But they are a disturbing influence and, if they were smart, they would pack up and go. But some people have thick skins). By and large I'm convinced that Floh will turn into a fellow who, as he further develops and matures, will be a factor within the Virginia group, somebody one may, or must, reckon with.

The last two Mohicans, Brötchen and Paul, are the most negligible members of the gang. Paul is nice, efficient, very comradely, and not very bright. He is the factotum around here, continuously bringing in the coal, somebody who could be exploited by anybody inclined to do so. When he claims, dead seriously (during a conversation about hotels), that the Aachener Quellenhof[47] is matchless in size, service, and beauty, it reflects not his low social background but, in my opinion, his immense naïveté, which permeates all he says and does. Wherever one places him he performs as best he can, and he's always the product of that environment that influences him at any given moment. As long as he is with G[ross]-B[reeseners] he will be perfectly useful and decent and a hundred percent reliable. And as he will be going with us, we can assume that this will indeed be the case.

There is nothing I can say about Brötchen, as I have not yet seen him out there [at the workcamp]. Here [in Amsterdam] he was the same peaceful citizen he has always been, somebody who will do his duty leisurely and phlegmatically and no more than that. [. . .]

With cordial greetings to you and Ernst Cramer,

Yours

---

29. CURT BONDY, AMSTERDAM, TO FREDERICK W. BORCHARDT, NEW YORK

February 9, 1939

Dear Borchardt.

I'm very sorry that we didn't meet in Europe. I got back from London yesterday and will probably go back to England again shortly to work in the transit camp.[48]

But today I am writing you about another matter and ask that you send an NLT [night letter telegram] to Gross-Breesen immediately upon receipt of this letter. The matter is as follows:

We can obtain a farm of 2,000 acres in Florida for the purpose of a settlement. It also appears possible to get the owner, whose name I don't know, to pay for the preparations and other costs. It would be necessary to make sure that the people get into the country. A banker, Hugo Kaufmann, is paving the way for this matter here. He's meeting the relatives of the owner in Monte Carlo soon and wants an outline from me.[49]

Today I pointed out to him the difficulties of getting people in, but told him that it may be possible for farmers to get the preference quota. I told him at the same time, however, that I didn't know whether the way this business was taken care of for our Virginia people can be generalized at all. I would have to get in contact with my American people on this business to find out whether such a proposal has any prospect of success. Mr. Kaufmann pointed out that since the land would be donated, no difficulties should arise in giving the people the land in individual shares, therefore choosing a similar method as for the Virginia people.

I am of the opinion that we absolutely must pursue this matter, all the more so as the ICA emigration to Argentina is now stopping. Without a doubt, we will easily be able to find a large number of well-trained farmers who would like *very much* to settle in America.

This question is not only important for [this] Florida [project], but is also decisively significant for the other agricultural projects in the USA. Please consider this matter very carefully. I don't need to write you about the horrible pressure we are now under in Germany, and how frightfully desperate the people are. My discussions in London and Amsterdam only convinced me that in spite of the goodwill of the people, the prospects for emigration are very poor. I expect your cable-answer in about nine days at the latest.

Sincerely yours

---

30. TÖPPER TO CURT BONDY

February 10, 1939

Dear Herr Bo!

It's not yet ten hours ago that you left, and I must write you again a more or less urgent letter. We have seen Karlsberg[50] and arranged with him that Dackel should go to Rotterdam to pick up the application forms there. Then we wanted to apply on Monday, with Karlsberg's help. Thus, Dackel went to Rotterdam and was told there that the [U.S.] consul was not yet sufficiently informed about us and would have to check with Berlin first. He was expecting further information about us from there, in which case he'll notify us. Before that we would not get any application forms and could not apply either. If we wanted to make the March deadline, the consul in Berlin would have to reply very soon. Thereupon we telephoned immediately with Stef, but he was not at home. We told his mother to notify you at once, before you go to see the consul [in Berlin]. I very much doubt that she managed this, but you must now try, come what may, to persuade the consul to reply to the inquiries of the consul here!!! Before that we cannot do anything and are powerless. Without a word from the consul in Berlin the consul [at Rotterdam] will do *nothing*.

We had also assumed that the consul [at Rotterdam] was better informed, and when we saw him the first time he did in fact convey this impression. But at the moment the situation is different again, and the man is apparently waiting for further details; so far he has only received our names. He probably also lacks any clear idea as to how the question of shares is being handled.[51] In any case, we hope very much that the consul will soon be notified so that we can make some progress here. Karlsberg is very nice, and is eager to help us. [. . .]

---

31. PROTOCOL OF A CONFERENCE OF CURT BONDY AND JULIUS L. SELIGSOHN WITH THE AMERICAN CONSUL IN BERLIN

February 15, 1939

VIRGINIA PROJECT

1. Present status: The Consulate requires officially certified report that the people in Gross-Breesen are especially well trained. Report will be turned in to the Consulate day after tomorrow.

2. The affidavits were all checked over today; minor additional information necessary for a few.

3. It hasn't yet been decided whether second request to Washington necessary. If request, then cable agreed upon.

4. The matter of girls: It is very unlikely that girls will be able to go along now.

5. Timing: Decisive answer from Washington expected at the latest within a few weeks (if request is even necessary). Seligsohn is to telephone a few days after submitting report.

6. People in Holland and Poland: We haven't inquired, since

preliminary questions have to be cleared up first. Request for notification of the two consulates will be made when the Berlin Consulate has basically approved it.

Postscript: Mr. Seligsohn sees the matter more favorably and requests the following additions to the protocol:

No. 4: "It was emphasized by us, in accordance with Mr. Thalhimer's wishes and his arrangement with the State Department, that the girls will not go to the farm. But the attempt will be made to procure individual emigration on agricultural preference quota for the girls."
The girls' papers were checked over just as [thoroughly as] those of the group were.

Bo

---

32. MEMORANDUM FOR THE FILE: CONSULTATION
AT THE AMERICAN CONSULATE, BERLIN

March 1, 1939

PRESENT: *Consul Norden, Consul Rose,*
Dr. Seligsohn, Dr. Bondy

A conference had apparently taken place before our arrival and part of a letter from the Consulate to the State Department in Washington was read to us. Inquiry about the contract, about the profitability of the farm. We must wait for the decision of the Department.

In case of refusal, our people must get to the USA by other means. Consul Norden said later in a private conversation: earliest date for trip across, April—latest date, August.

Letter goes on Monday, March 6 to USA.

Ingrid Warburg telegraphed Dr. Seligsohn, [asking] what is going on with Gross-Breesen; Thalhimer is getting uneasy.

Dr. Seligsohn is sending telegram and detailed written report to Thalhimer.

The consuls were quite friendly and helpful. I have the impression they want to help us, and in case a refusal comes from

Washington would handle us as if we had submitted affidavits in June 1938 without ado.

Re the Dutch,[52] I asked the consul: He said he couldn't give the consul in Rotterdam any instructions. I had the feeling, however, that they will most probably report to Rotterdam what they plan to do.

This business is unpleasant because we have to continue waiting, but I fully believe that the situation is not bad and that we should wait. I am not in favor of trying to send the eight boys who are still in Germany to England.[53] That is, I think we should do this: wait for an answer from Washington, which I expect at the latest in mid-April (we could perhaps try to request the answer from Thalhimer by wire).

The Dutch must, and anyway can, wait out this period of time. If the eight boys still in Germany were to go to the [Kitchener] Camp now, they would run the risk of getting numbers in England that wouldn't come up for two or three years, whereas now there is hope that in the case of refusal from Washington their turn will come up normally in July or August.

In the case of a negative answer from Washington the attempt would be made to get numbers for August in Berlin, with a special request for assignment to England, and then, since the camp requirements have been fulfilled, admission into Kitchener Camp.

For the four girls who are still here I recommend following through with the England plans.[54] There was no discussion of the girls or of individuals at all.

Gross-Breesen, March 1, 1939
Bondy

---

33. TÖPPER TO CURT BONDY

March 6, 1939

Dear Herr Bo!

Thank you very much for your news about America, even though it's not good. Now it means again waiting, waiting, and once again waiting; all we can do is hope that this time Washington will finally approve, and that it won't be another eternity.

Is there anybody over there who is pressing for a speedy decision, and will Thalhimer be doing something along this line?
[. . .]
    Should the desired notification from Was[hington] turn out to
be negative, then I am very pessimistic as far as the future of
us five is concerned. I do not believe that the consul here will
give us a [quota] number that will be called in the foreseeable
future. I already wrote you that all available numbers have been
transferred, for years ahead, to the [U.S.] consulates in Germany. It is not likely that the consul here [at Rotterdam], who
is very strict and unpleasant, will be as accommodating as the
one in Berlin, who has at least shown some traces of it. But there
is probably no use discussing these things now as we cannot
know at the moment how developments may go. I wish that we
could have you here again soon, and I herewith invite you most
solemnly to Wieringen for a "council of war" concerning the
emigration to America! Will you accept? [. . .]

Cordial regards
Yours

---

34. TÖPPER TO CURT BONDY

April 10, 1939

Dear Herr Bo!
    Here is the promised technical letter, adorned with especially
wide margins. I want to summarize as briefly as possible because
I know how little time you have. But please, do write me again
in spite of this.

    1. How are your plans progressing? Do you still intend to
leave for the USA within the next months? And what sort of
shape would that take?
    2. The day before yesterday I found out from Floh, who
visited me, that there has been a reply from the [U.S.] State
Department in regard to the matter of our "preference" in which
it stands by its decision of fall '38, thus presumably positive
and acknowledging. Now everything depends on the consul.

—Who will go on negotiating? Is anything at all being done? Do you know anything further? I have complained very vehemently that I have not been kept abreast of developments. I hope it will have some effect! I hope very much that this time a decision will be made for sure; for I believe that we cannot wait very much longer. Should everything fall through I shall write you in great detail and probably even shall come over [to England] for a personal meeting.

3. When will the circular letter be out? Will it materialize at all? I hear only very little from Breesen [. . .].

4. I had very interesting mail, probably a circular letter, from Haka [at Hyde Farmlands]. But it is always a little strange when the grapes are being dangled before one's mouth and one is forbidden to bite into them. For that's the way our American project looks. Well, wait and see! A familiar saying by now.

5. The international situation is deteriorating so much that one begins to think in terms of safety precautions for one's own dear self. We have discussed here often what to do in case war should break out and Holland is dragged into it; we have more or less reached the conclusion that the best thing would be to go to England. Would you please write to me and give your opinion on (a) whether one should get a visa for England, and how? (b) whether you think that it will be possible to enter England without a visa in case of an invasion [of Holland]? (c) or whether you consider all this simply a wild notion? I'm not very keen on being thrown into a Dutch internment camp, and the other Breeseners share this view. Then we'd prefer to get into your [Kitchener] camp.

6. Please do write to me, really, and give your opinion on both the Virginia situation and the general situation, and what we can conceivably do about the latter.

Otherwise I don't want to write anymore today. I wrote the letter in great haste and with interruptions, and as a result there are a lot of typos. Please, do write soon! I believe that I shall visit you yet in any case in your Jew camp.

For today best regards,

                                                            Yours

35. CURT BONDY, KITCHENER CAMP, ENGLAND, TO TÖPPER

April 12, 1939

Dear Töpper,

I have a very bad conscience that I still haven't written to you. I'll just dictate briefly now, and then add on a few personal lines [. . .]

About your questions:

1. My plans are not definite yet. I have to go to the USA within the next three months. Whether I come back again then is still uncertain.

2. A slight delay has occurred again in the Virginia business. Ernst is to report all the details to you. Thalhimer telegraphed that he is giving the required data to the State Department and that Seligsohn should wait for further news from him. I don't think the matter is going badly and I am quite hopeful.

3. The circular letter will be sent in the course of the week. I've already gotten a rough draft today.

4. The circular letter from Haka has also been sent to me.

5. I don't believe there is going to be a war now, and I think that if there were a war, we would have to count on much unpleasantness, in every nook and cranny, wherever we are. If some of you individually can get visas for England, so much the better.

6. Please thank Meui for his greetings. I don't know if it is right for me to give up my [Dutch] entry permit now; for example, in case of war it would be important for me to be able to go to Holland and have conferences at the American Consulate in Rotterdam. Think it over and then write me back.

Greetings,

Bo

36. TÖPPER TO CURT BONDY

April 30, 1939

Dear Bo!

This will be a technical letter today, though it won't be an easy one, as I shall raise a lot of questions, none of them being simple. But first the purely technical matter, the Australia project [. . . there follow details on the problems of how to book passage for the group].

It is terribly complicated and, above all, it does not look too good, since all the boats of the Slamat Line are booked full for June, and berths for July are going fast.

I didn't write you for such a long time because I expected every day to get some word on Virginia and had resolved at least to try to clarify the situation by the end of April. The situation is as follows: The Virginia project, according to reports from Seligsohn and Ernst Cramer, looks very bleak. Negotiations still revolve around the preference quotas, and on this issue S[eligsohn], judging from his letter, is not exactly very optimistic. Should the decision be negative, the attempt should be made to have those people who registered last year in Berlin [with the U.S. consulate there] placed on the August quota. I would not be among them, since the matter is even less clear in Holland; I have not been registered with the boys, and any intervention on the part of the consul in Berlin with the one here—if he would do it at all—would not include me. If I were to apply independently I have no idea how many years would pass before my turn came, especially since my [first] application at the time was rejected because my sponsor is no relative, and the wealthy sponsor [not a relative] did not satisfy the consul. Now the man here [consul] is already aware that I want to go to Virginia (we had seen him once, Dakel and I), and if I were to apply without the testimonial of the Berliner [consul] I would come again into conflict with the labor contract; thus, another and final rejection on the part of this pedant in Rotterdam would be very likely. What am I to do now? I'm afraid to keep on waiting for Virginia any longer, with prospects that it will materialize being low, because my passport, which cannot be extended, will expire within a year, and one does need some room for maneuvering. [. . .] If I were to know that Virginia would work out, let's say, by September—great! But the uncertainty whether it will work at all, and then the question, what next? You will say: "Töpper, you are basically still extremely well off. Look at my 3,000 unfortunate Jews many of whom have neither support from their parents nor a home nor anything, and who must also wait." —True, but nevertheless, this doesn't make me feel any easier, nor does it help to solve the personal questions I face. [. . .]

Last week I was in Wieringen again. I hitchhiked off in the evening, arrived at night, Friday night, and stayed until Monday morning. It is always good to be with the boys, and always depressing leaving them again and thinking over and reflecting on one's experiences. I had never realized how easily Jews can become proletarianized, that they can be so immensely ugly, internally ugly. Although I make allowances for the fact that they live in distress, as refugees, does this really mean that they must be apathetic, totally disinterested, discarding all basic rules of community and comradeship as soon as it becomes difficult to preserve them?

The nice thing is that the Breeseners, quite consciously and successfully, are fighting all this in their own ranks, but are they not merely a small fraction of these 300 people here? It's so sad and depressing when one has to watch how everything is being turned into something negative, a trait particularly common to Jews.

I always find people who look at everything in a Pollyannish kind of way stupid and shortsighted. At a time when not even the blindest of the blind can maintain any longer that we are the Chosen People, these apostles with rose-colored glasses claim that we have been chosen precisely for suffering—quite a mission, indeed. Bullshit with vanilla topping: we have failed all down the line; wherever one spits, there's one negative achievement after the next. That oh-so-much-touted world Jewry may be crying "shame!" and boycotting German goods, but beyond that, with a few exceptions, their fat behinds remain glued to their money bags. The committees may be full of good intentions, but since neither organization nor discipline are particularly pronounced traits of the Jewish people, they [the committees] let you down for the most part and are helpless as soon as they encounter the slightest obstacle. They always negotiate, but they never act. Whenever the going gets rough, the Jewish intellect vanishes, and what remains is a small, helpless little man who up to then has been all egghead. (Wieringen: 300 people, but [they are] too disinterested and incapable of creating a good intellectual climate around here. This will require people who have always been farmers and who must try to breathe some life into this joint. But even then it will remain questionable whether it [. . .] can succeed, for who can prevail against God, Novgorod, and intellectual narrowmindedness and debility!)

And what about the individual? Oh, it is useless and senseless to go into all this, because unfortunately one cannot change a thing, and to be continuously irritated is likewise pointless. After all, we are and shall remain a small but rather lousy lot and, God knows, I am right in the midst of it—am I even entitled to pass judgment?[55] [. . .]

Spring is a silly season, and everything is twice as difficult. It would be easier if I could see more clearly and had a more specific goal. [. . .] Would it be all right with you if I were to visit? [. . .] Are you mad at me now? Please write soon if you find the time and include something about your work and, above all, your future plans.

With my very best regards,

Yours

---

37. CURT BONDY TO JULIUS L. SELIGSOHN

undated; early May, 1939

Dear Mr. Seligsohn,

I received an express letter and telephone call from Gross-Breesen, as well as the letter from Haka from H.F. [Hyde Farmlands]. I don't know whether you are informed about the news that people with waiting list numbers who are outside the country are to be set back ten months for the benefit of those still in

Germany. Yesterday this same information was given to someone here at the London American Consulate General. I fear above
all that Thalhimer will abandon the project if our people get there
another half-year to a year later.

It is also important now that if the matter of preference [quo-
tas] in Berlin should work out after all, the consulate in Rotterdam be properly approached. Perhaps it will be possible for you
to arrange something along this line while in Holland. The news
of the delay of departure for those outside the country [Germany]
has caused severe consternation here, too. Emigration is looking
altogether very gloomy from here.

If you want to talk to me about the Virginia affair or other
questions, I could come to Amsterdam without any difficulty. I
still have a London-Amsterdam plane ticket.

Sincerely yours,
Bo

---

38. CURT BONDY TO TÖPPER

May 3–4, 1939

[. . .] About your personal affairs:

Yesterday we received a letter from Haka from which we see
that the report has still not gone off to the Immigration Department. I wrote immediately to Ernst C[ramer] and asked him to
contact Thalhimer quickly, by lettergram, to prompt him to send
the report to Washington at once, and to make sure that the [Ber-
lin?] consulate is informed of this as soon as possible. [. . .]

I see Virginia positively; a wait of one month; then, if necessary, further attempts. [. . .]

May 4th [handwritten]

Dear boy, I am on the train to London in order to meet with
Dr. Otto Hirsch. Meanwhile encl[osed] letter came from Seligsohn. You can see from it that my optimism is not entirely un-
justified. But we must wait.

Man, I am not mad at you in the least because you're applying
pressure, and I understand you *very* well. To be sure, this eternal
wait is not very pleasant, but I hope that we'll see more clearly,
perhaps very clearly, within a few weeks, one way or other. And
then we'll be able to discuss everything in person. Okay? —I'm
traveling through a countryside in bloom, and soon *our* country
will be there, too, and we shall rebuild, and train people, and
shall demonstrate that the Jews need *not* be a small but rather
lousy lot (*kleines aber mieses Völkchen*). Are the Gr[oss]
Bre[eseners] lousy? *Were* they really *so* different when they came
to us? As you know, I am an optimist even when it comes to
pedagogic matters!

Thus to repeat: *Make the best of it! And keep smiling!* [In English in the original.]

It would be great if you and the other two could visit here,
but an overnight stay is not exactly easy because other people
are not allowed to have visitors for an extended period of time
either. I'm just a little adjutant and must first ask my director.*
Well, it's not *merely* technical and social work, but *mostly*. I
have now started a workshop entitled "Knowing People" [*Menschenkunde*], which will become "Knowing Life" [*Lebenskunde*]. We thereby concentrate on people from the youth movement and especially those from the youth groups (*Bund*). Scheier
and the two boys are doing well. Scheier worked until today as
a "commoner": digging, washing dishes, etc. But today he was
"discovered," and now it's all over with the *privacy*. [Last word
in English.]

So, as usual: Chin up!

Affectionately,
Yours Bo

*When are you coming? Write me the particulars in advance.

39. TÖPPER TO THE GROSS-BREESENERS

MANUSCRIPT FOR "BRIEFE AN DIE ALTEN GROSS-BREESENER,"
UNPUBLISHED

AMSTERDAM
June 24, 1939

[. . .] The last thing that still comes to my mind is our present situation and each individual's attitude to it. Unfortunately we are all—despicable word[s]—refugees, emigrants, fugitives. To some extent our lives don't look worse than, for instance, in Gross-Breesen (I mean here "socially" speaking), but some of us have now become servant girls or farmhands, and there are some who find their position depressing. I believe that all of us would feel that way, that we would hurt inside, somehow, if we had to sit and eat in someone's kitchen and were given to understand at times that one is nothing but a "refugee." Many of the—to us "foreign"—employers possess sufficient tact and intelligence to judge people by their behavior. In those cases our boys and girls can live as in paradise. But some people get the notion that they have already done a good deed by taking a given individual into their home and cannot understand how hard it is for that person when he notices that his benefactor is not overly concerned about him but considers him part of the household equipment and merely expects him to live up to his duties. After all, he, the benefactor, has done the same! There is nothing one can do about this but resign oneself. We are, alas, dependent today, at least externally, and only in time will we become once again free and independent persons. But it is sad, and above all, wearing, if one is constantly made to feel that one must show "gratitude." But we ought to be quite clear in our minds who we are and what we want to become, and should try to learn to keep smiling in the face of such treatment. Only if deep down inside ourselves we stand above the situation shall we be able to handle things and to extract the positive aspects from it. One can learn everywhere and in every situation. Those of you who know me will be aware that I, of all people, would find it hard [to cope with such a situation] and, surely, shall find it hard someday. But I am determined that once that happens I shall think of what I wrote here, and then things will be much easier. Nobody is actually "degraded" until he truly believes he is and then behaves accordingly in attitude and manner. But until it happens—no way! [. . .]

---

40. FAREWELL AT ROTTERDAM (BY TÖPPER)

AMSTERDAM
June 11, 1939

It is Friday, June 9, 1939. I get the impression that Rotterdam is populated exclusively by Gross-Breeseners. They arrived this morning, two batches from Germany, one person from Brussels, three from Amsterdam. Rotterdam shows them a rather pleasing side. For the most part it's sunny and pleasantly warm, and one does not notice overly much the gray ugliness of the district where our quarters are. Dackel and I are here as representatives of the "Dutch" Breeseners,[56] and tonight Bo plans to come from Berlin by air. 15 Breeseners, 13 boys and 2 girls, plan to depart tomorrow on the Dutch boat *SS Slamat* for Australia.

Our headquarters is in the "Hammelburg." It is by no means an old citadel from the wars of the *Gueux*,[57] but the name of the Jewish owner of a hostel (*Pension*) who will provide the group with food for the day. Blackhaired, sly, and busy, he seems the figure of Shylock personified. Despite his friendliness I cannot detect any warm feelings for him in my heart, for instinctively I always hear the sentence: "I'll have his heart!" But he takes good care of us, and that's all that matters. The group is lodged in three boardinghouses and there's a lot of "commuter traffic" between the St. Laurenskerk and the Oppert. The Hammelburg serves only meals.

With the arrival [of the group] at the station this morning, everything is busily in motion. The first thing is to take care of the technical stuff like passports, steamship tickets, and luggage. We stand crowded in a small, dark passage of the Hammelburg among pieces of luggage, overcoats, and hats. A gentleman from the committee stands impatiently below, waiting for Dackel and Pitt, who are supposed to accompany him with the passports and steamship tickets. It's difficult to find one's things in the cramped mess. Herko's steamship ticket cannot be located at first; it has disappeared. Together, they both search through his stuff. As always in circumstances like these, Dackel sweats from aggravation and curses like a Berlin garbageman. The gentleman from the committee states every two minutes categorically that his time is limited and that he must leave. In that rush I actually manage to break one of the ashtrays Mrs. Hammelburg had recommended to our particular care. Töpper! [means: clumsy]. But in the end everything surfaces, the two disappear with those papers and the man-in-a-hurry, and we are assigned to our respective quarters.

Okay, we finally have some peace. I take turns sitting in different rooms that the boys and girls may not leave for the time being as they have no passports, and we talk. They tell me about Breesen and the trip to this place. I report about the farewell of the four "Australians" from Wieringen, who just now must be boarding their boat; about Holland; about myself. While we're talking I suddenly say to myself: "Lord, I'm still sitting here now, talking, getting to meet some of these boys for the first time, and being glad of it; or meet up with others again, as the case may be. And tomorrow morning they'll have left for the other end of the world, for Australia!" Indeed, we live in mad times, for on top of everything we must rejoice that they can go to Australia at all! —After everything has been taken care of and the paperwork is quite in order, we have time to ourselves. Some go to the movies, for the first time again after a long interval, and the rest, Dackel and I among them, go for a walk, look at the harbor, talk, and try not to think about the fact that tomorrow at this time they will all be gone.

At 10 P.M. we all stand at the small pavilion of KLM, the office of the Royal Dutch Airlines, and wait for Bo's arrival. When he steps off the bus that has brought him from the airport into the city, the passersby watch, curious and excited: "Who might this be, this gentleman surrounded by young people, whose

142   THE GROSS-BREESEN DOCUMENTS

welcome is blocking traffic?" But as soon as they realize that he's not the Queen of Holland they move on without having solved the puzzle. Those who still want to talk with Mr. Bondy accompany him, and the rest of us go in small groups through the city at dusk and, for the last time, sit down together in a cafe. We only return to our boardinghouses at midnight. For the [Australia] group it will be the last night on European soil.

And now the moment has come! We all stand in front of the *Slamat*, a not-too-large boat of the Rotterdam Lloyd [steamship line]. Suddenly Floh and Prinz show up, too; they've hitchhiked here. Around 10 A.M. we all go on board. For many it is the first big boat they have seen. I, too, have never been on a large ocean steamer, except for ten minutes on the *Hamburg*. It's a strange feeling to walk around in a house that swims. The stewards are nearly exclusively Malayans or Javanese. While we're standing in one of the cabins I notice something going on behind me. When I turn around, there is one of the stewards, who had entered noiselessly. They wear sandals on their feet, on their heads a kind of turban, altogether a curious, strange picture. I am reminded of Wiechert's *Geschichte eines Knaben*[58] when I watch these brown people with their large, dark animal eyes. They do not understand English, nor German either. It will be a strange thing for the boys to be served by these silent, sound-less people! The entire ship is crowded with German and Viennese emigrants. A sad, somehow depressing sight to watch some of these, partly rather old, people depart for a country that they will never really understand, whose language they will never really learn to speak properly, and that lies many thousand miles away from where they were born. Australia! For these people it is indeed the end of the world.

One feels more comforted when one watches the Breeseners who will travel along. They all are confident, and who of us would not be? I suddenly get the strong urge to go with them, not to have to leave the boat again. And yet, I know that in a few hours the signal will be given that will separate all of us, probably for a long time, perhaps forever.

Upstairs on the promenade deck of tourist class we all get together once more. There are no farewell speeches, nor does

Bo say anything about what he expects from this group. We are Breeseners, we trust one another, have confidence in our work and our objective. As we stand there we know that we belong together. Mountains of farewell notes are being penned. The mood is by no means sad. Only occasionally, someone glances surreptiously at his watch and mumbles: "Dammit!"

"Only a week ago we sang:

> And it soon will be true
> that we stand by the sea
> and think of the distant homeland;
> for the little troop intensely prepares
> to abandon the old gray stone walls.
> Nothing keeps us anymore.
> Overjoyed we'll leave shore;
> soon our sails will flutter eastward,"

one of them says to me as we both stand by the rail for the last time. I merely nod. If you only knew how much I want to come along!

And still the boat doesn't move. We're standing below now, on the quay, and they are up there on deck. Fifteen Breeseners, our first, large, united group: Pitt, Herko, Erich, Leo, Klaus, Werner, Spitz, Wachsi, Franz, Erwin, Fritz, Hans, Herbert, Hanni, and Inge. Almost none of them are older than seventeen. And in Colombo they will be joined by Johnny, Posche, Bosi, and Rudi. One of them has fetched his accordion, and now they're singing. They are songs we sang in the *Bund* [youth group], and later at Breesen: "The gray fog," "When shall we meet again, companions?" "We shan't budge nor falter, we want to stand together! . . ." And then: "Who'll go along to Australia, when no one's in command? . . ."

Now the last hawsers are loosed. Even the gangway of First Class, which had been left to the last, is now being pulled on board. Slowly, very slowly the little tugboat pulls the steamship into the center of the river Meuse. The last verbal exchanges to and fro. Once again they're singing, but the sounds become increasingly faint. We have gotten out our handkerchiefs and are waving. To make this recognizable from far away we're waving

in unison. Bo commands: "Up! Wait! Down! Up! Wait! Down!"
The group that stands at the ship's sternpost waves back the same
way. Now they become smaller and smaller, less and less clearly
recognizable. And finally one sees only the ship as it moves
slowly but steadily down the Meuse. It is to bring our friends
to their new destination.

Fifteen Breeseners go to Australia; five Breeseners walk slowly
back into town.

---

41. FROM THE DIARY OF GÜNTHER MARCUSE

THE NEW FACE OF THE LABOR CAMP

Tuesday, October 6, 1942

It has been obvious to us at the labor camp [at Gross-Breesen]
for over a year now that some day we would have to leave the
manor house (*Schloss*) where we have been living. With the arrival of the painters, we were presented with a *fait accompli* as
they proceeded at once to renovate the manor house. The result
was that one room after another had to be vacated. [. . .]

Wednesday, October 7, 1942

Until now, whenever we spoke of moving, the reference was
only to the beds. Today we worked first of all on setting up the
rooms, as not everything could be left in the trunks. We did what
we could to equip the individual rooms with wooden closets,
cupboards, and wall shelves. The transport of these objects took
place throughout lunchtime and again in the evening after work.
Needless to say, nothing could be moved during working hours.
[. . .]

Sunday, October 11, 1942

Not even on Sunday did we have enough time to put things in
order; instead, we had to glean potatoes in the morning.

Monday, October 12, 1942

We were permitted to take with us from the library books that have been used a lot, because it [the library] will be closed down on account of the renovation. With the work inside the manor house proceeding at a rapid pace, the girls also had to vacate their rooms as of noon. [. . .]

Tuesday, October 14, 1942

The farm management received two telephone calls. The first, from the labor exchange, inquired whether preparations had been made to receive prisoners of war (Russians!). The second call came from the District Economic Office, which informed us that we would be no longer permitted any wheat products, and that we must obtain our bread against ration coupons instead of continuing to rely on our own. [. . .]

October 17–18, 1942

The farm manager went home for the weekend. On Sunday morning, as usual, we worked.

Monday–Tuesday, October 19–20, 1942

On Monday, the first infirmary worker, a girl, arrived for kitchen duty. On both days, a scheduled visit by the supervisory authorities failed to materialize.

Wednesday, October 21, 1942

At noon the Gestapo announced their arrival. Shortly before the workday ended, the entire camp assembled in the manor house, and Gestapo official Hampel announced the tentative separation of the camp['s Jewish workers] by name. All married couples as well as the girls and several boys, 22 people altogether, are to leave Gross-Breesen on October 31. They will go together, as a group, for [forced] labor service to Grüssau.[59] The Gestapo anticipates that the remainder will follow sometime later.

Sunday, October 25, 1942

The farm manager deemed it necessary to have us work the entire day.

Since the beginning of food rationing we Jews have had to do without our meat ration altogether. Besides, we are now entitled to only one loaf of bread.

The people who are to leave here have used their free time every day for packing.

Thursday, October 29, 1942

After difficult preliminary negotiations it became possible to obtain for the people [about to depart] a wagon for stowing their heavy baggage.

Friday, October 30, 1942

After supper, the farm manager called everybody together for the purpose of saying goodbye to the people.

Saturday, October 31, 1942

In contrast to previous alarms, which until now could be immediately blocked by appeals, today our friends of whom we have become fond over the past years have left us. [. . .]

At 4 A.M. the entire camp was on its feet, and the horse-drawn carriage that was to take the people to the train also stood ready. Everybody helped to load the hand baggage, and we said good-bye. Whoever had not yet realized what this particular leave-taking signified soon became aware of it once the people had left. [. . .]

Sunday, November 1, 1942

In the morning we worked (7–1). The farm manager was away.

Monday, November 2, 1942

[. . .] With the return of winter standard time, working hours have been fixed at 6:30 A.M. to 11 A.M., and 1 P.M. until shortly after 5 P.M. (dusk).

Tuesday, November 3, 1942

The first reports have arrived from Grüssau; for the initial phase they sound surprisingly positive.

Saturday, November 7, 1942

Mr. Zimmer[60] once again visited the estate. In addition, the farm manager raised a lot of hell. He wanted to exploit a piddling incident to deprive us of [today's] supper, but revoked his decision after we appealed to Mr. Zimmer. During supper he announced that he had succeeded with great difficulty in procuring for everybody an extra loaf of bread per week. He also offered us horse meat. [. . .]

Saturday, November 14, 1942

With all the harvest chores behind us and despite the reduction in the work force, three [of our] people could be assigned once again permanently to the cowbarn.

Sunday, November 15, 1942

[. . .] Mr. Hildebrand [the farm manager] left for home. Furthermore, the rearrangement of rooms that began a few days ago was completed today. [. . .]

Saturday, November 21, 1942

The manor house was made ready for inspection, and 110 beds were installed. Inspection by three higher-grade Army officers.

Sunday, November 22, 1942

Because of the sudden onset of frost during the night we all had to work from 9 to 11 A.M. to cover a potato pit, and this despite the so-called day off. [. . .]

Wednesday, November 25, 1942

In the evening a woman "Eastern worker" (*Ostarbeiter*) (Russian) arrived for cleanup work in the manor house. She is the first one sent here by the Labor Exchange.

Friday, November 27, 1942

The weather turned milder again, so that we can go on with the plowing. The Army inspected the manor house the second time around and arrived at a decision as to use and furnishings. [. . .]

Monday, November 30, 1942

After he had obtained specific information, the farm manager forbade us henceforth to boil down any more sugar beets [for making syrup], claiming that we stole them. He let the kitchen crew boil down the remainder for the community at large. [. . .]

Tuesday, December 1, 1942

Three soldiers arrived as an advance detail for the future military hospital Breslau XI, hospital branch Gross-Breesen. [. . .]

Wednesday, December 16, 1942 [in the original, 17]

The farm administration had a hog slaughtered for the farm manager, owners, and employees. In the afternoon there was a visit from the Gestapo, who discussed our situation over a good meal.

Sunday, December 20, 1942

Cleanup of the farmyard by way of punishment because of a misunderstanding that arose during plowing on the Fuchsberg [field].

Monday, December 21, 1942

Mr. Zimmer spends his first night at Gross-Breesen.
    The farm manager gave permission . . . to boil down the remaining beets for Christmas.

Wednesday, December 23, 1942

The farm manager is leaving on vacation until December 29. We, too, spent a pleasant holiday.

Saturday, December 26, 1942

After a long interval we played soccer once again.

Sunday, December 27, 1942

The remaining mattresses were exchanged for straw pallets.

Monday, December 28, 1942

In the afternoon, Mr. Zimmer showed up with the intention of staying until New Year's Eve. Inspection of the estate by an inspector of the Land Settlement Association [*Landsiedlungsgesellschaft*] of Silesia on behalf of the HTO.[61]

Tuesday, December 29, 1942

The farm manager arrived this afternoon, rather late.

Friday, January 1, 1943

We had an uneventful New Year. We all hope to be able to stay here for a long time yet. [. . .]

Tuesday, January 12, 1943

As a start, the hospital receives eight wounded [soldiers]. The administration is headed by a managing director with the rank of lieutenant. We probably cannot count on the soliders for help with the work, as all of them are amputees of either the arms or the legs.

Friday, January 15, 1943

The manor house is declared off limits for us. We have petitioned [farm manager] Hildebrandt about the food.

Saturday, January 16, 1943

Special roll call for all people: "You have complained about the food, that the food has deteriorated. That's absolutely outrageous. On the contrary, now that the military is here, Mrs. Posner can run the kitchen better than ever. I have been a soldier myself long enough. To insult a German woman that way, this won't go unpunished. You know that in addition to the four pounds of bread a week to which you are entitled, I have arranged that you'll get gruel in the morning; that's 200 pounds a month—I ought to go to the penitentiary for that. From now on you'll get only what's coming to you: four times turnips, three times potatoes." . . . He [farm manager Hildebrandt] forbids us to have warm suppers and demands that the petitioner apologize to Mrs. Posner.

Tuesday, January 19, 1943

So far, no more soup in the morning, no more warm suppers, so that we have to secure provisions on our own. Cottage cheese has also been eliminated. The weekly ration amounts to 125 grams fat and 175 grams jam. [. . .]

Friday, January 21, 1943

The usual supper. An announcement by the farm manager. Besides some phrases about the work, he said: "If you are getting food again you can thank Mrs. Posner, who interceded on your behalf. Starting Monday, you'll also be getting soup again in the morning. On the other hand, you'll be getting only 100 grams of fat; the rest Mrs. Posner needs for cooking so the food won't burn. If that doesn't suit you, you can go without any food. Thus thank Mrs. Posner; had it been up to me, you would have gotten nothing."

Saturday, January 23, 1943

One by one, more wounded are arriving. Contrary to our assumptions stated earlier, the wounded are passing time in the farmyard by various attempts at work. [. . .]

Wednesday, February 3, 1943

Following a lengthy conference among Mr. Hildebrandt, Zimmer, and Roth, as well as several other gentlemen from the HTO and the Silesian Land Settlement Bureau, Mr. Zimmer was removed from his job. Mr. Salbach, Director of the Land Settlement Bureau, will take over the operation of the farm as provisional administrator. The actual operation will be under the control of Inspector Mende [from] Peneschen.

The conference about this takeover lasted for ten hours.

Friday, February 5, 1943

Mr. Mende arrives with a bookkeeper, a woman, to examine the books.

Tuesday, February 9, 1943

Mr. Salbach, accompanied by the managers Hildebrandt and Mende, inspects the farm and discusses with them the upcoming important jobs. In the process they also discussed the question of manpower. They reached an agreement to the effect that they would apply to the Gestapo for a return of the 14 [Breesen] friends from Grüssau.

Friday, February 12, 1943

Our circle of friends anxiously awaits this decision because, first, the labor camp Grüssau is in the process of being dissolved, and they [the inmates] are already slated for transfer to the East [*Osteinsatz*]. Second, if the decision should be favorable, it would mean that our stay here would be assured for an extended period of time.

Saturday, February 13, 1943

The managers have returned and informed us that the recall [of the 14] has no chance of succeeding.

Thursday, February 18, 1943

Upon our return from work we learned that the Labor Exchange has informed the farm management that the Gross-Breesen estate will be assigned 40 workers from the East. The Jewish component is to leave two days later. (Completed the fourth year at Breesen. G. M.).

Friday, February 19, 1943

The manager had to pick up the 40 people in Burgweide, near Breslau. They were quartered above the chicken barn and in the former Kindergarten . . . We await the decision about our fate, which is in the hands of the Gestapo.

Saturday, February 20, 1943

Mr. Mende reported that the Gestapo had not yet reached a final decision and that we could take a holiday until Monday, March 1.[62]

Friday, February 20, 1943

The tremendous tension that had prevailed all week was still further heightened by the news that Mr. Hampel has returned from Grüssau earlier than expected. Reached by telephone, he announced that a final decision would be taken by Saturday or Sunday, or that the Gestapo would show up on Monday morning. Whatever happens, though, the half-Jews would remain at Breesen. This prompted the manager to revise the work schedule, and he'll have the half-Jews trained in . . . office work and running of the store room.

Those who had gone on holiday for the weekend returned ahead of time, since a police raid had unexpectedly been staged in Breslau earlier in the morning under the direction of the Vienna Gestapo. We forego a more detailed description at this point: their conduct is sufficiently well known to us from Berlin. The raid included all full Jews [*Volljuden*].

Prospects of an extended stay are diminishing for us. Filled with apprehension, we await further developments.[End of diary.]

Notes

1. ON THE SITUATION OF JEWISH YOUTH UNDER HITLER

1. However, various restrictions on Jewish activities were imposed on the local levels as early as February 1933; see Joseph Walk, ed., *Das Sonderrecht für die Juden im NS-Staat,* pp. 3 ff. The Civil Service Law, euphemistically entitled "Law for the Restitution of Professional Public Service," initially exempted non-Aryan officials who had been in public service prior to August 1, 1914, or who had fought in the front lines during the First World War (*ibid.,* p. 12). The exemptions were obtained through petitions by Jewish organizations to Reich President von Hindenburg. After his death in August 1934, the exemptions were no longer honored.

2. Helmut Genschel, *Die Verdrängung der Juden aus der Wirtschaft;* Karl A. Schleunes, *The Twisted Road to Auschwitz.*

3. The two best accounts on this issue are still Schleunes, *The Twisted Road,* and Uwe Dietrich Adam, *Judenpolitik im Dritten Reich.* A more recent publication that grew out of an international conference held in West Berlin, October 28–31, 1985, and sponsored by the Leo Baeck Institute, New York, with the participation of the institute's London and Jerusalem branches, sheds light on the general situation of the Jews at that time: Arnold Paucker, ed., *Die Juden im nationalsozialistischen Deutschland— The Jews in Nazi Germany, 1933–1943.* Half the contributions are in English. On the gradual strangulation of Jewish life in Germany see also Jacob Boas, "The Shrinking World of Germany Jewry, 1933–1938." Equally relevant are the various contributions in the sections entitled "Die Verfolgung der Juden" and "Vertreibung und Exil" in Ursula Büttner, ed., *Das Unrechtsregime,* volume 2. My comments on the general situation of Germany's Jews after 1933 owe much to all these studies.

4. See, for example, "Anordnung Nr. 63/65 der Reichsleitung der NSDAP vom 11. April 1935 mit Anschreiben des Reichsinnenministers vom 15.6. 1935," reprinted in Günther Rehme and Konstantin Haase, . . . *Mit Rumpf und Stumpf ausrotten . . .,* pp. 69–71; "Der Reichs- und Preussische Minister des Innern an die Landesregierungen [and] (für Preussen: die Herren

156   NOTES: ON JEWISH YOUTH UNDER HITLER

Ober- und Regierungspräsidenten), vom 20. August 1935," BA (Bundesarchiv) Koblenz, R 58/276, no. 26 (also in Rehme und Haase, *ibid.*, p.
67); and "Der politische Polizeikommandeur der Länder [Werner Best]:
An alle Politischen Polizeien der Länder, vom 19. Dezember 1935," BA
Koblenz, R 58/276, no. 34. All three documents pertain to the matter of
"individual violence" (*Einzelaktionen*).
    5. Genschel, *Die Verdrängung*, p. 60.
    6. See, for instance, Ian Kershaw's "Antisemitismus und Volksmei-
nung. Reaktionen auf die Judenverfolgung," in Martin Broszat and Elke
Fröhlich, eds., *Bayern in der NS-Zeit*, 2:294–95; and *ibid.*, 1:427–86,
passim. See also Ian Kershaw, *Popular Opinion and Political Dissent in
the Third Reich: Bavaria*, pp. 231–77, passim.
    7. "Arbeitsbericht der Reichsvertretung der Juden in Deutschland für
das Jahr 1937," pp. 2–9, mimeographed. Hereafter ARV; Rosalyn Manowitz, ed., *Reflections on the Holocaust: "Kristallnacht,"* pp. 18, 43, 84–
85; Hans Winterfeld, "Deutschland: Ein Zeitbild 1926–1945," *passim*.
    8. For examples see Manowitz, *Reflections*, pp. 54, 60, 73, 85, 94, 99,
101, 133; Winterfeld "Deutschland," 80–91, 99, 113, 133; Hans Rosenthal, *Zwei Leben in Deutschland*, p. 31; Inge Deutschkron, *Ich trug den
gelben Stern*, pp. 17, 47–48; Joel König, *David*, pp. 72 ff.
    9. Gert-Julius Herrmann, "Jüdische Jugend in der Verfolgung," pp. 25,
35; see also König, *David*, Deutschkron, *Ich trug den Gelben Stern*, and
Valentin Senger, *Kaiserhofstrasse 12*, all passim. All three authors, who
survived the Nazi persecution underground, came from poor families.
    10. There were many others like them, especially in Berlin, who were
able to survive for this reason.
    11. ARV 1937, p. 4; 1938, p. 48.
    12. The Reichsvertretung was founded on September 17, 1933. It was
the first such organization in the history of Jews in Germany that could
speak for, and represent, all Jewish groups, non-Zionist and Zionist alike.
After passage of the Nuremberg Laws in September 1935, the Reichsvertretung had to change its name to Reichsvertretung der Juden in Deutschland (National Representative Agency of Jews in Germany), as Jews were
henceforth no longer first-class German citizens and thus no longer permitted to call themselves "German" Jews.
    After the November 1938 pogrom, in July 1939, the Reichsvertretung
was forced to adopt the designation Reichsvereinigung der Juden in
Deutschland (National Association of Jews in Germany) and from then on
became virtually a mere tool of the Gestapo. It had lost its formerly still
considerable freedom of action in representing the interests of Germany's
Jewish community. On Reichvertretung and Reichsvereinigung, see the
contributions by Herbert A. Strauss and Otto D. Kulka, respectively, in
Paucker, ed., *Die Juden*, pp. 125–52, 353–63; and Friedrich S. Brodnitz,
"Memories of the Reichsvertretung," pp. 267–77. All three studies list
older and also some more recent material published on the subject.

13. "Arbeitsbericht des Zentralausschusses für Hilfe und Aufbau bei der Reichsvertretung der Juden in Deutschland [Berlin], 1933," p. 26; hereafter Adz.

14. Georg Josephthal, "Die Berufsfrage der jüdischen Jugend," p. 40. Josephthal, then a Jewish functionary of the Zionist Palestine Office (*Palästinaamt*), subsequently of the Reichsvertretung, estimated in February 1938 that of the 85,000 Jewish youths, 40,000 were born between 1913 and 1923. See the same author, "Pädagogische und auswanderungspolitische Gesichtpunkte," p. 6.

15. Herrmann, "Jüdische Jugend," pp. 15–16, 74.

16. Quoted in Adam, *Judenpolitik,* pp. 68–69. The election campaign referred to pertains to the last "free" national election to parliament (*Reichstag*) in Germany until the end of the Third Reich, the election of March 5, 1933.

17. *Reichsgesetzblatt 1933,* 1:225 ff.; Bruno Hoffmann, "Die Ausnahmegesetzgebung gegen die Juden," pp. 72–73; Walk, *Sonderrecht,* pp. 17–18. For this and the following see also Walk, "Jüdische Schüler an deutschen Schulen in Nazideutschland."

18. AdZ 1934, 2:24. See also Charles Hannam, *A Boy in That Situation.*

19. See, for instance, Deutschkron, *Ich trug den gelben Stern,* pp. 23–24.

20. Winterfeld, "Deutschland," pp. 42–43, 49–60, passim.

21. Manowitz, *Reflections,* pp. 8, 41, 59–60.

22. Senger, *Kaiserhofstrasse 12,* p. 83; but see also pp. 55, 76–84.

23. Geert Platner et al., eds., *Schule im Dritten Reich,* p. 47. For a general background on German schools and their educational system during the Nazi years: Harald Scholtz, *Erziehung und Unterricht unterm Hakenkreuz,* with excellent bibliography; and Norbert Franck and Gesine Asmus, eds., *Heil Hitler, Herr Lehrer.*

24. Platner, *Schule im Dritten Reich* p. 50, and also pp. 129–77, passim, where several Jewish former students relate their experiences in school during the thirties.

25. AdZ 1933, pp. 25–28; ARV 1937, pp. 54–55. See also Walk, "Jüdische Schüler"; Salomon Adler-Rudel, *Jüdische Selbsthilfe unter dem Naziregime 1933–1939,* both passim.

26. ARV 1937, pp. 2–9; 1938, pp. 18–20; Josephthal, "Berufsfrage," p. 40.

27. Winterfeld "Deutschland," p. 76.

28. König, *David,* pp. 77–78.

29. Deutschkron, *Ich trug den gelben Stern,* p. 26; cf. pp. 222–48. Walk, "Jüdische Schüler," and Adler-Rudel, *Jüdische Selbsthilfe,* pp. 19–46.

30. Martin Buber, "Wie erziehen wir ein unbefangenes, unabhängiges neues Geschlecht?"

31. AdZ 1933, p. 27; *Anhang* (Supplement) to AdZ 1934, vol. 1. Le-

158   NOTES: ON JEWISH YOUTH UNDER HITLER

schnitzer (1899–1980) emigrated in 1940 to the USA, where he taught at several institutions and where he published a number of books. He also taught after the Second World War as guest professor at the Free University, Berlin (West). Some of the best-known German postwar scholars of German-Jewish history today were initially trained in Leschnitzer's seminar.

32. Käthe Rosenheim, "Jüdische Sozialarbeit in Deutschland als Einheit," p. 94.

33. Heinemann Stern, *Warum hassen sie uns eigentlich?* p. 194; AdZ 1935, pp. 125 ff.; Josephthal, "Berufsfrage," p. 41; Landenberger, "Die soziale Funktion," p. 99.

34. Manowitz, *Reflections,* p. 84 (but see also p. 14).

35. Rosenthal, *Zwei Leben,* p. 38.

36. Herbert Freeden, "A Jewish Theatre Under the Swastika"; see also by the same author *Jüdisches Theater in Nazideutschland.*

37. For a treatment of the German *Bünde* and a survey history of the German youth movement in general, see Walter Z. Laqueur, *Young Germany: A History of the German Youth Movement,* pp. 155–66 and passim.

38. Chaim Schatzker, "Martin Buber's Influence on the Jewish Youth Movement in Germany." On the Jewish youth movement as such, see Hermann Meier-Cronemeyer, "Jüdische Jugendbewegung."

39. "Tätigkeitsbericht des Reichsausschusses der jüdischen Jugendverbände," in Reichsausschuss, *Gemeinschaftsarbeit,* pp. 84–86; also Brodnitz, "Jüdische Sozialarbeit," pp. 269, 271, 275.

40. "Lageberichte der Gestapostelle Potsdam für Juli und September 1934," Geheimes Staatsarchiv Berlin-Dahlem, Rep. 90 P/2,5, no. 76, H 3, and no. 78, H 1. For a brief analysis of the nature of these Gestapo reports see my article "Die 'Judenfrage' im Spiegel amtlicher Berichte 1935."

41. "Tagesbericht der Gestapostelle Frankfurt a.O. vom 30. August 1935," Geheimes Staatsarchiv Berlin-Dahlem, Rep. 90 P/2,3, no. 83, H 4.

42. On the partiality of the Gestapo toward Zionists see Hans Mommsen, "Der nationalsozialistische Polizeistaat"; Angress, "Die 'Judenfrage,'" p. 24; Jehuda Reinharz, "Hashomer Hazair in Nazi Germany," p. 326. On Schwarzes Fähnlein see Carl J. Rheins, "The Schwarzes Fähnlein, Jungenschaft 1932–1934"; and Meier-Cronemeyer, "Jüdische Jugendbewegung," pp. 105–6.

43. Landenberger, "Die soziale Funktion," p. 100.

44. How strongly the Reichsvertretung was committed to advance emigration, and for this purpose tried to secure as many suitable training facilities as possible, is evident from the "Arbeitsberichte" or "work reports" (AdZ 1933–1936, ARV 1937–1938). For the role that the Jewish youth movement played in promoting and running special occupational training facilities see Landenberger, "Die soziale Funktion," pp. 99–106, but also the more critical assessment of Josephthal, "Berufsfrage," pp. 40–48. On the general debate in the Jewish press over whether or not to emigrate

during the first two years after Hitler came to power, see Herbert Freeden, "Bleiben oder Gehen."

45. Ernst Wiechert's books were very popular among German adolescents, including Jewish ones, during the 1930s. For a discussion of the impact that "blood and soil" romanticism had on German Jews, especially the Zionists, see George L. Mosse's chapter "The Influence of the Volkish Idea on German Jewry," in his *Germans and Jews*, pp. 77–115.

46. Ernst G. Lowenthal, "The Ahlem Experiment." Friedel Homeyer, *Beitrag zur Geschichte der Gartenbauschule Ahlem 1893–1979;* and Carl J. Rheins, "German Jewish Patriotism," pp. 43–46, 220–21.

47. AdZ 1933, p. 28. Italics mine.

48. AdZ 1935, pp. 124–30, 139.

49. "Akten des Preussischen Ministeriums des Innern (Staatssekretär Grauert)," n.d., p. 150, and in *ibid.*, "Bericht des Landrats in Cottbus," November 17, 1933, pp. 151–53, both in Geheimes Staatsarchiv Berlin-Dahlem, Rep. 77, no. 31; and "Lageberichte der Gestapostelle Frankfurt a.O., Tagesbericht vom 5. Juli 1935," Rep. 90 P/2,3, no. 81, H 4.

50. "Geheime Staatspolizei: Judenfrage, Emigration 1934–1937," vol. 1, Geheimes Staatsarchiv Berlin-Dahlem, Rep. 90 P/58, vol. 1, H 1, pp. 67–72.

51. "Lagebericht der Gestapostelle Potsdam für Juli 1935," Geheimes Staatsarchiv Berlin-Dahlem, Rep. 90 P/2,4, no. 82, H 9.

52. The Reichsnährstand, founded by the NSDAP on September 13, 1933, included most Germans involved in agriculture, both farm owners and employees. It supervised production and distribution, set marketing regulations, and acted also as the agency that represented the interests of Germany's agricultural population. It operated under the guidance of Reichsbauernführer Walter Darré, Reichminister for food supply (*Ernährung*) and agriculture. See Horst Giess, "Die Rolle des Reichsnährstandes."

53. AdZ 1935, p. 127; 1936, p. 137.

54. AdZ 1935, p. 141.

55. AdZ 1935, pp. 142–43; 1936, pp. 152–53. ARV 1937, pp. 83, 88, 92 ff.; 1938, pp. 37–38. Adler-Rudel, *Jüdische Selbsthilfe,* pp. 192–202, lists all training facilities in operation on December 31, 1937, and on pp. 202–4 he discusses the general state of training and preparation for emigration as of June 30, 1939.

56. Josephthal, "Berufsfrage," p. 40; Landenberger, "Die soziale Funktion," p. 104; AdZ 1936, p. 151; Adler-Rudel, *Jüdische Selbsthilfe,* pp. 97–102, 114–16; Meier-Cronemeyer, "Jüdische Jugendbewegung," p. 107. Jehuda Reinharz has recently stated that "the total number of German children who came on *Youth Aliyah* [to Palestine] between 19th February 1934 and 1st October 1939 was 3,437." Reinharz, "Hashomer Hazair," p. 334. For the beginnings of Youth Alijah see Eva Michaelis Stern, "Erinnerungen an die Anfänge der Jugendalijah in Deutschland."

57. Josephthal, "Berufsfrage," p. 43. For figures on Hachsharah training see Reinharz, "Hashomer Hazair," p. 327.

58. Josephthal, "Gesichtspunkte," p. 13, and "Berufsfrage," pp. 41–44; AdZ 1935, p. 131. A former Gross-Breesen trainee of the "third generation" wrote recently in a letter to a friend: ". . . I arrived in Gross-Breesen in January 1940, at a most unpromising time. The winter was very severe, and consequently all the plumbing in the manor house (Schloss) was frozen. There was very little heat. . . . The main reason that I stuck it out then was the fact that I had been begging my parents since 1936 to let me go to Gross-Breesen. For reasons known only to them, my parents refused until there was almost no other way for me to escape a draft into temporary forced labor. . . ." Letter, Irmgard Muller to Ernst Cramer, January 4, 1987. Copy in the author's possession.

59. Perez Leshem, Strasse zur Rettung 1933–1939; Adler-Rudel, Jüdische Selbsthilfe, pp. 204–15; Meier-Cronemeyer, "Jüdische Jugendbewegung," p. 107; Joergen Haestrup, Passage to Palestine; Gertrude van Tijn, "Werkdorp Nieuwesluis."

60. Landenberger, "Die soziale Funktion," p. 103.

61. Josephthal, "Gesichtspunkte," pp. 4–6, and "Berufsfrage, pp. 42–43.

62. Rudolf Melitz, ed., Das ist unser Weg, pp. 14, 23.

63. Ibid., p. 27.

64. Ibid., p. 69.

65. Winterfeld, "Deutschland," pp. 135–36.

66. Rosenthal, Zwei Leben, pp. 41–42.

67. König, David, pp. 115–21, 135–37. Quotation is on p. 117.

68. Werner T. Angress, "Auswandererlehrgut Gross-Breesen," Annelise Ora Borinski, Erinnerungen, 1940–1943, p. 22.

69. König, David, p. 173.

70. Borinski, Erinnerungen, p. 25. In 1948, Hatikvah became Israel's national anthem.

71. This is not the place for a lengthy discussion of "Crystal Night." The following three studies are useful: Hermann Graml, Der 9. November 1938. "Reichskristallnacht"; Lionel Kochan, Pogrom November 10, 1938; and William S. Allen, "Die deutsche Öffentlichkeit und die 'Reichskristallnacht.'"

72. Anon. [Günter Friedländer], Jüdische Jugend zwischen Gestern und Morgen.

73. Ibid., p. 7.

74. Ibid., pp. 26–27.

75. ARV 1938, p. 3; Adam, Judenpolitik, pp. 226–32.

76. Manowitz, Reflections, pp. 94, 133.

77. Herbert A. Strauss, "Jewish Emigration from Germany," pp. 313–28; Herrmann, "Jüdische Jugend," p. 74.

78. Strauss, "Jewish Emigration," pp. 317–28; ARV 1938, p. 48; Adler-Rudel, *Jüdische Selbsthilfe*, pp. 216–19.

79. Adler-Rudel, *Jüdische Selbsthilfe*, pp. 216–19, 97–102.

80. *Ibid.*, pp. 209, 218; ARV 1938, pp. 11–12; Herrmann, "Jüdische Jugend," pp. 70–99. See also Esther J. Baumel, *The Rescue and Resettlement of the Jewish Refugee Children from Europe.*

81. Deutschkron, *Ich trug den gelben Stern*, p. 50.

82. Manowitz, *Reflections*, p. 95.

83. *Ibid.*, p. 63. For the mass deportations of Jews from Baden and other parts of southwestern Germany on October 22, 1940, see Raul Hilberg, *The Destruction of the European Jews*, pp. 392, 402; and Robert O. Paxton and Michael R. Marrus, *Vichy France and the Jews*, pp. 10–11.

84. Adler-Rudel, *Jüdische Selbsthilfe*, p. 219. On Himmler's ban of emigration for Jews see Walk, *Sonderrecht*, p. 353.

85. On Shanghai see David H. Kranzler, *Japanese, Nazis, and Jews*, and Marvin Tokayer, *The Fugu Plan.* Additional studies on this particular Jewish "refuge" are in progress.

86. On Aliyah Beth see Jon and D. Kimche, *The Secret Roads;* Leshem, *Strasse zur Rettung*, pp. 84–85; König, *David*, pp. 106–7, 130–33, 146–47; van Tijn, "Werkdorp Nieuwesluis," p. 169.

87. Unless otherwise noted, the following account is based on Meier-Cronemeyer, "Jüdische Jugendbewegung," pp. 114 ff.; König, *David*, pp. 134–67, passim; and Borinski, *Erinnerungen*, pp. 18 ff.

88. The exact date and the circumstances under which this decree came into being are both a matter of dispute. See Bruno Blau, *Das Ausnahmerecht für dis Juden in Deutschland, 1933–1945*, p. 86; Walk, *Sonderrecht*, pp. 336–37, 354; and Adam, *Judenpolitik*, pp. 285–92.

89. Internationales Militärtribunal (IMT), *Der Prozess gegen die Hauptkriegsverbrecher vor dem Internationalen Militärgerichtshof*, 42 vols. (Nuremberg, 1947–49), vol. 26, Doc. 710-PS, pp. 266–67. See also Adam, *Judenpolitik*, pp. 306–8.

90. *Reichsgesetzblatt* 1941, 1:547.

91. Walk, *Sonderrecht*, p. 353.

92. Hans Buchheim et al., *Anatomie des SS-Staates*, 2:373, 380.

93. Borinski, *Erinnerungen*, p. 21. The reference here is to a familiar headline in the Zionist newspaper *Jüdische Rundschau* of April 4, 1933, in which its then editor-in-chief, Robert Weltsch, commented on "Boycott Day" (April 1). The headline read: "Wear it with pride, the yellow badge!"

94. König, *David*, p. 164.

95. *Ibid.*, p. 166.

96. *Ibid.*, pp. 178–79.

97. Deutschkron, *Ich trug den gelben Stern*, pp. 89, 95–108. Needless to say, these lists of property enabled the local Nazi authorities to pick and choose from the belongings listed once the former Jewish owners had been deported.

98. Borinski, *Erinnerungen*, pp. 24–25.

99. On Jewish resistance see Konrad Kwiet and Helmut Eschwege, eds., *Selbstbehauptung und Widerstand;* Arnold Paucker and Lucien Steinberg, "Some Notes on Resistance"; and Margot Pikarski, *Jugend im Berliner Widerstand*. The "White Rose" and the "Group Herbert Baum" were both composed primarily of young people. The Baum group was overwhelmingly Communist and Jewish. The White Rose, which originated on the campus of Munich University and is mostly remembered today for its two principal founders, Hans and Sophie Scholl, had a largely Catholic membership with supporters on several German university campuses. For the latter group see Inge Scholl, *The White Rose*, and Hermann Vinke, *The Short Life of Sophie Scholl*.

100. Walk, *Sonderrecht*, p. 379.

101. König, *David*, pp. 191, 195.

102. Homeyer, *Beitrag*, pp. 129, 150–64.

103. This emerges from the last entry, on February 26, 1943, in the diary of a Gross-Breesen trainee, Günther Marcuse. See the English translation by Joseph Walk, "The Diary of Günther Marcuse." Large sections of the diary are reprinted here as document 41 in chapter 3.

104. Herbert (Ehud) Growald, "Hachschara und Hachscharazentren in Deutschland, 1940–1943," *Jad Waschem 01/241*, as cited in Meier-Cronemeyer, "Jüdische Jugendbewegung," p. 115, n. 17. When I saw the documentary film *Shoah* a year after the German edition of this book was published, I realized that this seems to have been a common gesture among the Polish peasants working along the railway tracks that led to Auschwitz and the other killing centers.

2. GROSS-BREESEN TRAINING FARM

1. I published an article on Gross-Breesen over two decades ago; see Angress, "Auswandererlehrgut Gross-Breesen."

2. Friedrich S. Brodnitz, "Die Reichsvertretung der deutschen Juden," p. 109; "Arbeitsbericht des Zentralausschusses," passim; hereafter ARV.

3. *Jüdische Rundschau*, no. 4, January 14, 1936 ("Unbegreifliches . . .").

4. *C. V.-Zeitung*, no. 4, January 23, 1936, and no. 23, June 4, 1936. The board of trustees was composed of men and women prominent in Jewish affairs. Though it would serve little purpose to list them here, the interested reader may consult Angress, "Auswandererlehrgut Gross-Breesen," footnote 12. On Seligsohn, see his brief biographical sketch in Ernst G. Lowenthal, ed., *Bewährung im Untergang*, pp. 155–57; on Schwarzschild, see *Lexikon des Judentums* (Gütersloh, 1967), p. 738; on Bondy, see the next note. It should be noted that two major Jewish organizations— the Reichsbund jüdischer Frontsoldaten (RjF), or League of Jewish War Veterans, and the Bund deutsch-jüdischer Jugend (BdjJ), or League of Ger-

man-Jewish Youth, the largest German-Jewish youth organization—as well as the widely read "assimilationist" *C. V.-Zeitung* were prominently represented among the men and women who founded the emigration training farm: Dr. Leo Löwenstein and Dr. Curt Elsbach of the RjF, Heinz Kellermann and Martin Sobotker of the BdjJ, and Dr. Alfred Hirschberg of the *C. V.-Zeitung*.

5. For background information on Bondy, see Herrmann A. L. Degener, ed., *Wer ist's?* 9th ed. (Berlin, 1928), p. 165; Ernst G. Lowenthal, ed., *Juden in Preussen*, p. 34; Werner Kindt, ed., *Die deutsche Jugendbewegung, 1920–1933*, p. 1757.

6. The German Ministry of Agriculture and especially the Reichsnährstand demanded that only "Jewish" farms should serve as training centers for "non-Aryans" (ARV 1936, p. 137). Thus, the fact that the farm ultimately chosen was legally owned by (non-German) Jews undoubtedly facilitated the process of securing the final approval of the Reichsnährstand.

7. *C. V.-Zeitung*, no. 20, February 20, 1936. The business office was located adjacent to the central offices of the RjF at Kurfüstendamm 200, in Berlin, where the author of this book worked as an assistant from early April until early May, 1936. Some of the following information is therefore based on personal recollection.

8. According to Mr. Arie Goral, originally Arie Sternheim, now residing in Hamburg, Germany (FRG), from approximately 1931 Gross-Breesen was a Zionist Hachsharah center and continued to function in this capacity until at least 1933. Information based on a letter by Mr. Goral to Professor Dr. Werner Jochmann in Hamburg, who communicated this information to the author.

9. "Bericht des Kuratoriums des Jüdischen Auswandererlehrgutes Gross-Breesen an die Mitglieder des Kuratoriums des Jüdischen Auswandererlehrgutes Gross-Breesen," Berlin, June 23, 1938, p. 4 (File Fritz Schwarzschild, mimeographed); hereafter "Bericht des Kuratoriums." See also Alfred Hirschberg's report, "Zwischenwelt im Werden," *C. V.-Zeitung*, no. 23, June 4, 1936.

10. On *Baurat* Jacoby's observations on his function at Gross-Breesen see Regierungs- und Baurat R. Jacoby, Berlin, "Erfahrungen beim Aufbau eines Auswandererlehrgutes," *Jüdische Wohlfahrtspflege und Sozialpolitik. Blätter der Zentralwohlfahrtsstelle und der Abteilung Wirtschaftshilfe bei der Reichsvertretung der Juden in Deutschland*, n.s. (Berlin 1937), 7:49–51.

11. Bondy in *C. V.-Zeitung*, no. 17, April 28, 1938.

12. On the question of the girls and related aspects, see Curt Bondy's letter to a mother, dated July 3, 1936: "Die 'Mädchenfrage' in der Umschichtung," in Rudolf Melitz, ed., *Das ist unser Weg*, pp. 81–85.

13. *C. V.-Zeitung*, no. 4, January 23, 1936; no. 23, June 4, 1936.

14. After the Second World War, Cramer became Associate Editor of *Die Neue Zeitung*, the official organ of the American occupation force, in

Munich. He is today with the Axel-Springer-Verlag in the Federal Republic of Germany.

15. "Gross-Breesen Letter 18," April 1949, pp. 1–5, and "Gross-Breesen Letter 20," November 1956, pp. 2–5, both mimeographed. These circular letters, the headings of which changed over time from German to English, were sent between July 1938 and November 1956 (with some additional ones sent sporadically until the 1980s) to former trainees and friends of Gross-Breesen. They contain mostly letters and essays by former trainees, usually with a short introduction by Bondy, Cramer, or both. Originally entitled "Briefe an die alten Gross-Breesener," the heading changed to "Gross-Breesen Letters" after Bondy moved to the United States in 1940. A set of these mimeographed circular letters (1938–1956) is deposited with the archive of the Leo Baeck Institute in New York City.

16. See Bondy's unpublished, mimeographed brochure "Boys and Girls, a Discussion," Autumn 1939, and an essay by him on the same topic in "Achter Brief an die alten Gross-Breesener," March 1940. The latter gives a good insight into the way in which this problem was handled at Gross-Breesen. Today, this "policy of self-denial," as it may be called, may seem overly severe. But given the fact that any scandal arising, for instance, from a teenage pregnancy would have done great damage to an institution such as Gross-Breesen in light of the prevailing reluctance of parents to send their daughters to training centers in the first place, Bondy's at times fanatical insistence on "chastity" becomes at least understandable.

17. For a more detailed treatment of this question see "Gross-Breesen Letter 18," April 1949, pp. 3–5.

18. In May 1986, during a reunion of former Gross-Breesen trainees and friends in Israel to commemorate the fiftieth anniversary of the founding of the training farm, many of the men and women now in their sixties and seventies smiled knowingly whenever the word *Bewusstmachung* was mentioned.

19. See, for instance, *C. V.-Zeitung*, no. 23, June 4, 1936.

20. Pym (Paul Yogi Mayer), "Gross-Breesen im Aufbau. Jüdisches Auswandererlehrgut eröffnet," *Der Schild*, May 29, 1936.

21. The author of this book did not; the *Ober* kicked him out after a couple of weeks for "insubordination," and he came close to being expelled from Gross-Breesen.

22. "Bericht des Kuratoriums," June 28, 1938, p. 4.

23. "Gross-Breesen Letter 20, November 1956, pp. 3–4.

24. Karl Neumeyer is the son of Alfred N., for many years a prominent judge at Bavarian courts, and from 1929 to 1933 a high judicial official (*Oberstlandesgerichtsrat*) in Munich. He was also an active and leading member of Munich's Jewish community, and his son, nicknamed "Wastl," was brought up in the traditional religious home of his parents. The entire family emigrated in 1938, before the November pogrom, to the Jewish settlement Avigdor in Argentina (discussed later). After Alfred Neumey-

er's death, Karl, his wife Lisbeth, and their children moved to Israel, where they still live today. See Monika Richarz, ed., *Jüdisches Leben in Deutschland*, pp. 358–66, esp. n. 15.

25. Letter, Curt Bondy to Fritz Schwarzschild, April 29, 1938. The relevant passage reads: ". . . You saw in G.B. a perhaps last opportunity . . . for realizing your very pronounced hopes of [creating] a fundamental religious Jewish attitude. The Jewish [non-Zionist] youth movement [to which Schw. had once belonged] suffered shipwreck in this respect, and there now seemed to arise a new opportunity for realization [of your hopes]. No doubt, G.B. has failed to fulfill your wishes and hopes in this matter—has proved unable to do so. I am aware of it . . . and am myself saddened as a result. I am strongly convinced that [for this reason] the Gross-Breeseners will lack an ultimate basis of support and, just because of this, I am not at all certain whether they will prove themselves." The late Fritz Schwarzschild kindly put that letter at my disposal. See also "Gross-Breesen Letter 20," November 1956, pp 3–4, 21–22.

26. Friedrich S. Brodnitz, "Die Reichsvertretung der deutschen Juden," pp. 108–9.

27. Personal communication, Fritz Schwarzschild to author, approx. 1946.

28. ARV 1936, p. 18, mentions the efforts of the Reichsvertretung in this respect. A "Nova Breesen" exists today in Rolandia, Paraná, the name of a plantation owned by a former Breesen trainee whose widow still runs it. It was the only such project that materialized in Brazil as a result of the "Paraná Plan."

29. For further details of this particular project, including some comments on the work of the Jewish Joint Distribution Committee and related matters, see the chapter 3 and corresponding notes. The plantation in Virginia, "Hyde Farmlands," was the only large-scale settlement (roughly 35 people) that eventually materialized. But its existence, in part because of the effects of the Selective Service Act, was short-lived; by the spring of 1941, the last of the Breesen settlers had left the farm.

30. *C. V.-Zeitung*, no. 17, April 28, 1938. HICEM was an acrostic of HIAS (Hebrew Immigrant Aid Society), ICA (Jewish Colonization Association), and EMIGDIRECT (*Emigrationsdirektorium*, or managing board for emigration).

31. "Vierter Brief an die alten Gross-Breesener," March 1939, p. 4.

32. For details see the first three "Briefe an die alten Gross-Breesener," July, August, and October, 1938, respectively; also *C. V.-Zeitung*, no. 17, April 28, 1938.

33. See the London *Times* of November 12, 1938, p. 12, with the statement that the events surrounding the assassination of vom Rath had gotten "scant notice" in the German press.

34. This account relies heavily on the reports of former Gross-Breeseners, some of whom provided them (orally) immediately after their release from Buchenwald and their subsequent emigration to Holland. In addition,

the author has used recollections of former Breeseners written much later, e.g., Ernst Cramer, "Ein Amerikaner in Buchenwald," p. 8, and a letter from "Prinz" to the author, dated September 20, 1981 (hereafter "Prinz" Report). A brief notice on events in Gross-Breesen was published on November 12, 1938 in the Dutch working-class newspaper *Het Volk*.

35. "Prinz" Report.

36. On this topic see Lionel Kochan, *Pogrom*, pp. 54–58, 76 ff.; Hermann Graml, *Der 9. November 1938*, pp. 28–29; Eugen Kogon, *Der SS-Staat*, pp. 209–10; Kogon, *The Theory and Practice of Hell;* Falk Pingel, *Häftlinge unter SS-Herrschaft*, pp. 93–94, 265, note 126. There are several indications that such an *Aktion* had been considered by the government for quite some time, although perhaps not to the extent of the one that occurred in November 1938. For some preparations had been made, among them, for instance, the construction of the auxiliary barracks 1A to 5A in Buchenwald, which on November 9, 1938 were still not completed; they were separated from the rest of the camp by barbed wire. After completion of the *Judenaktion* they were torn down again, on February 15, 1939.

37. Besides the pertinent studies listed in the preceding footnote, see also *Konzentrationslager Buchenwald;* Moritz Zahnwetzer, *KZ Buchenwald;* Julius Freund, *O Buchenwald;* and Walter Poller, *Arztschreiber in Buchenwald.*

38. "Prinz" Report.

39. On the camp command structure at Buchenwald see BA (Bundesarchiv) Koblenz, Sammlung Schumacher, no. 329. On Hackmann see Zahnwetzer, *KZ Buchenwald*, p. 36 and Poller, *Arztschreiber*, p. 153–54.

40. "Prinz" Report.

41. Cramer, "Ein Amerikaner in Buchenwald."

42. During the first few days after the wave of arrests there were already at least 70 cases of nervous breakdown. After the termination of the *Judenaktion*, several hundred Jews had died in Buchenwald.

43. This punishment, which in German was called *"über den Bock gehen"* (lit.: to go across the [saw]buck), was administered on a special wooden rack to which the delinquent was strapped on his stomach, head down and legs drawn forward, exposing the naked buttocks. The *Bock* was used in all concentration camps. Kogon, *Der SS-Staat*, pp. 108–9, Poller, *Arztschreiber*, pp. 121–29.

44. For the situation on hygiene, see Freund, *O Buchenwald*, pp. 53–54; *Konzentrationslager Buchenwald*, p. 27, and Kogon, *Der SS-Staat*, p. 210.

45. Kochan, *Pogrom*, pp. 146–50; Adam, *Judenpolitik*, pp. 204–32; Schleunes, *The Twisted Road*, pp. 245–54.

46. Gross-Breesen Letter no. 18, April 1949, p. 1.

47. See chapter 3, document no. 1.

48. Van Tijn, "Werkdorp Nieuwesluis," pp. 193–94.

49. See document no. 40 in chapter 3.

50. This is based on the address lists in the fifth and seventh letters to the old Gross-Breeseners as compiled in July 1939 and January 1940.

51. The following comments are based primarily on subsequent written accounts by former Gross-Breeseners, except for Günther Marcuse's diary (on which see the introductory remarks to chapter 3). The entries make it possible, at least for the last few months of the existence of a group of (former) Breesen trainees, to check the subsequent reports of survivors against the contemporary record of Marcuse. These are the reports by former members of Gross-Breesen's "third generation" who survived: Klaus Freund, "Gross-Breesen Letter" no. 11, October 1941, pp. 14–16; Alfred Cohn, *ibid.*, no. 16, June 1946, pp. 5–6; Henny Weiss, *ibid.*, no. 17, June 1947, pp. 17–18. See also the testimony of Arthur Wolff at Yad Vashem; a letter from Ernst G. Lowenthal to Curt Bondy, October 10, 1947, and a letter from Gerda Guttmann to Ernst G. Lowenthal, November 5, 1941, both in E. G. Lowenthal's private archive in Berlin. Despite some minor discrepancies on details, notably dates and numbers, the various testimonies agree on all essential points, which has made it possible to reconstruct the final phase of Gross-Breesen and the fate of the last generation of its trainees at least in bold outline.

52. "Gestapo-Befehl II B 4–1937/41," cited in Walk, ed. "The Diary of Günther Marcuse," p. 164, note 22. The official dissolution of the emigration training center by which the Jewish personnel became subject to Gestapo supervision and control (and we can assume that by then the nominal supervision of the Reichsvereinigung that existed earlier was terminated as well) has been confirmed by Hans Hirsch, Gerda Guttmann, and Arthur Wolff. Some additional information on life at Gross-Breesen until the spring of 1941 was provided by Ms. Irmgard Muller, a former trainee and survivor, in an interview with the author on October 18, 1986. The Gestapo order II B 4-1937/41 merely established de jure what had existed de facto for months prior to the official dissolution.

53. See chapter 3, document no. 41, entries of January 15, 16, and 19, 1943.

54. Lazarett XI, Breslau, Teillazarett Gross-Breesen; see chapter 3, document no. 41, entry of December 1, 1942.

3. THE GROSS-BREESEN DOCUMENTS

1. Gertrude van Tijn, "Werkdorp Nieuwesluis"; See also H. B. J. Stegeman and J. P. Vorsteveld, *Het Joodse Werkdorp in de Wieringermeer 1934–1941.*

2. Töpper's account, here and elsewhere, is not always entirely accurate as to details. But when he wrote, his only sources of information were the media and reports of refugees who had fled to Holland.

3. The Obersalzberg was a place and mountain east of Berchtesgaden

where Hitler owned a large villa and where he spent a good deal of his time.

4. Sala was a former Breesen trainee. *Het Volk* was a Dutch working-class newspaper.

5. This remark pertains to the efforts by American Jewish relief organizations to persuade the U.S. Department of State in Washington, D.C. to instruct the U.S. consulate in Berlin to issue agricultural "preference visas" to Gross-Breesen's "Virginia group." (See also note 41 below for further details.)

6. William B. Thalhimer, department store owner in Richmond, Virginia, who purchased the estate Hyde Farmlands for Gross-Breesen's "Virginia group."

7. Frederick (originally Fritz) W. Borchardt, 1901–1956, was a businessman in Germany who emigrated to the United States in 1937 and there worked for the National Refugee Service in New York.

8. Another reference to the effort to get American agricultural "preference visas."

9. Heinz Kellermann, b. 1910, Doctor of Law, leader of the youth group Ring, Bund [deutsch]-jüdischer Jugend, 1934–1937. He emigrated to the USA and lives today in Maryland. Haka, a former Breesen training assistant, was then already at Hyde Farmlands.

10. This assumption ultimately proved correct, although the writer of these lines could not possibly have known this when he wrote the letter.

11. Dr. Fritz Bondy, a chemist, was Curt Bondy's younger brother.

12. Also "Holland Committee" or just "committee": "Het Comitee voor bijzondere Joodse Belangen," a service committee for Jewish refugees from Germany and Austria. It was located in Amsterdam. A suborganization, "Stichting Joodsche Arbeid," administered from 1934 the "Werkdorp Nieuwesluis," Nieuwesluis Workcamp, near Wieringerwaard in northern Holland. It functioned as an agricultural training farm and transit camp for Jewish refugees from Germany and, after March 1938, from Austria as well. They were expected eventually to move on either to Palestine or to other countries overseas. See van Tijn, "Werkdorp Nieuwesluis," and Stegeman and Vorsteveld, *Het Joodse Werkdorp*.

13. Hilde Meyrowitz, a social worker.

14. National Coordinating Committee for Aid to Refugees and Emigrants Coming from Germany. This American Jewish service organization for German refugees existed from 1934 to 1939.

15. Two training assistants and four trainees went to Kenya; see chapter 2.

16. Dr. G. T. J. de Jongh.

17. Stroppen was a small place near Gross-Breesen; the farm's telephone exchange was located there.

18. Dr. Ingrid Warburg, born 1910, worked with several service organizations in New York, among others with the National Council of Jew-

ish Women, the American Jewish Joint Distribution Committee, and the National Coordinating Committee. Daughter of Fritz M. Warburg, co-owner of the Hamburg bank M. M. Warburg & Co. After the firm had been "aryanized," Fritz Warburg emigrated to Sweden but returned to Hamburg in the fall of 1938 in order to settle the affairs of the Jewish Hospital there. Arrested, he was not released until May 1939, when he returned to Sweden.

19. Organized by the Reichsvertretung; see Baumel, *Rescue and Resettlement.*

20. Gertrude van Tijn was Secretary of the Wieringen Committee. The reference is to the admission of all released Breeseners to the Nieuwesluis Workcamp. See van Tijn, "Werkdorp Nieuwesluis" for her recollections of this period.

21. The title of Lion Feuchtwanger's anti-Hitler novel was subsequently changed to *Geschwister Oppermann* (*The Oppermanns*). It was published in 1933.

22. George van den Bergh: Professor, Chairman of the Wieringen Committee ("Stichting Joodsche Arbeid").

23. ICA: Jewish Colonization Association (also JCA) founded in 1891 to help Jews who had fled from eastern Europe to relocate overseas in settlements especially established for them. Some Breeseners went in 1938/1939 to the ICA settlement "Avigdor" in Argentina, as is discussed in chapter 2.

24. Bondy was, in fact, in Buchenwald, and the report of a man who knew Fritz Bondy's cousin and who claimed to have been imprisoned with Curt Bondy was false. Rumors such as these abounded.

25. Early in July 1938, there was still approximately 550,000 Jews in Germany and Austria combined. Austria had been annexed in March of that year.

26. All three trainees mentioned held Polish citizenship and thus became victims of the deportation of Polish Jews on October 28, 1938. See also document 1.

27. Fritz Schwarzschild, 1896–1967. From 1926 to 1928 Executive Director of the Association of Jewish Youth Clubs in Germany (Verband der Jüdischen Jugendvereine Deutschlands); 1930–1936, founder and director of Jewish Farmwork, Inc. in Berlin (Jüdische Landarbeit GmbH); 1936–1938, the responsible official for group emigration with the Reichsvertretung and Treasurer (*Finanzreferent*) for Gross-Breesen. Emigrated in January 1939 to France, in August 1939 to the USA. In New York, co-founder of Congregation Habonim.

28. Dr. David Warmbrunn, 1879–1942. Chemist, from 1936 the director of a chemical laboratory in Amsterdam. Emigrated in 1940 to Portugal, in 1941 to USA.

29. This proved wrong. Two Breesen boys were not released until the end of 1938 and early 1939, respectively.

30. This Denmark emigration project never materialized.

31. No communal settlement was ever realized in Australia.

32. Hopes to find temporary places of work for some Breesen trainees in Denmark could not be realized.

33. A group of Breesen trainees, who called themselves after their former group leader, nicknamed Hannio; he had died early in 1937. They all shared one room together. Most groups in Gross-Breesen were named after the person who was in charge of them and their respective room.

34. Trainees who died in Gross-Breesen in 1936 and 1937, respectively; two died through accidents, one committed suicide.

35. Martin Gerson, 1902–1944. Bachelor of Science in agronomy. From 1924 manager of the experimental estate Bärenklau, near Berlin. Subsequently teacher at the Jewish gardening school (*Gartenbauschule*) at Ahlem; 1930–1933, at the Jewish communal settlement Gross-Gaglow. After 1933 Director of the Hachsharah Winkel Estate and from 1941 of Neuendorf Estate. Gerson was actively engaged in helping the Gross-Breeseners and also trainees from other training centers who had been arrested in the wake of Crystal Night to be released from concentration camps. He was eventually deported to Theresienstadt and perished in Auschwitz.

36. All these arrangements turned out to have been tentative. Thus, E. Cramer went to Virginia, not Kenya, and many other changes were made as well.

37. Dr. Otto Hirsch, 1885–1941, *Ministerialrat* (ministerial counselor), 1933 Executive Director of the Reichsvertretung of Jews in Germany. Perished in the Mauthausen concentration camp.

38. Martin Sobotker, 1899–1977; legal assistant, 1933–1939; director of youth welfare service (*Jugenpflege- und Jugendwohlfahrtsdezernat*) of the Berlin Jewish community; 1935–1939, member of the board of trustees for Gross-Breesen. In January 1939 he emigrated to Sweden, and in October 1939 to the USA. From 1939 to 1941 he was a farmworker at Hyde Farmlands, Virginia, and from 1946 to his death, executive director of Congregation Habonim in New York City.

Dr. Alfred Hirschberg, 1901–1971, was after 1933 chief editor of the *C. V.-Zeitung* and legal advisor (*Syndikus*) to the Centralverein deutscher Staatsbürger jüdischen Glaubens (Central Association of German Citizens of Jewish Faith); 1939 emigration to France, 1940 to England and then to Brazil.

39. Dr. Julius L. Seligsohn, 1890–1942, lawyer, director of the Hilfsverein der Juden in Deutschland (Society to Aid Jews in Germany); member of the executive committee of the Reichsvertretung and member of the board of trustees for Gross-Breesen. Perished in the Mauthausen concentration camp.

40. Hannah Karminski, 1897–1942; social worker, general secretary of the Jewish League of Women, staff member of the Reichsvertretung. Perished on the way to one of the extermination camps.

41. With the enactment of the Immigration Act of 1924 the USA established annual immigration quotas for the different countries. After 1933, the German quota was no longer sufficient to accommodate the number of applicants, so that the waiting lists grew longer and longer. The much-desired exceptional permission for immediate immigration was generally granted to academicians and artists invited by certain American institutions, people with special skills, e.g. farmers, or very wealthy people. To those, preference visas were issued.

42. In order to obtain permission to immigrate to the United States for those Breeseners who got stranded in Cuba, Holland, or Poland.

43. Probably the Kitchener Camp, situated in the south of England, where Bondy was temporarily a leading staff member.

44. Scheier's replacement was a manager named Dingethal; see chapter 2.

45. Prinz went to Hyde Farmlands, Virginia after all.

46. A reference to Bondy's weekly inspection—on Sunday mornings —of the trainees' wardrobes at Gross-Breesen.

47. The Aachener Quellenhof was a fifth-rate inn in Aix-la-Chapelle (Aachen).

48. Probably the Kitchener Camp.

49. The Florida project never materialized.

50. Dr. Bernhard Karlsberg, lawyer. After leaving Germany he specialized as a counselor on emigration in Amsterdam.

51. See document 25. According to U.S. immigration law at that time, nobody could enter the country if he or she had a work contract, except for artists and academicians especially invited by American institutions. To get around this particular obstacle, the Gross-Breesen trainees going to Virginia were given shares in the ownership of the farm, Hyde Farmlands.

52. The reference is to the Breeseners in the Nieuwesluis Workcamp.

53. They were able to emigrate to Virginia in the summer of 1939.

54. Those girls who had been trained in Gross-Breesen were to go to England as household servants. Most of them were able to realize this plan. Some subsequently moved on to the United States.

55. These derogatory comments about the people at the Nieuwesluis Workcamp (except for the Gross-Breesen contingent there) and about Jews in general may shock many readers today, and understandably so. How can one today explain these remarks then made by a young Jew? There were, of course, the atmosphere and the general pressure of the moment that evidently affected him as he wrote the letter. The despair, anxiety, and depressed mood that these lines reveal may well account for his intolerant views about some of the people he encountered in the workcamp, though in particular about those Jews abroad from whom he expected help and who, he obviously believed, let him and his friends down.

His clear rejection and hatred of National Socialism and all it stood for are evident from his entries in his diary, notably the initial ones. On the other hand, there is some indication that the Nazi *Zeitgeist* had taken hold of him, too, at least partly, as it affected other young Jews at the time as well. This was especially true for those who, like the writer of this letter, had gone to a non-Jewish state school during the early years of the Third Reich, and there had absorbed, probably more or less subconsciously, some of the Nazi prejudices (sexist and racist as well as anti-Semitic). Finally, the very elitist attitude that affected some of the young people who had gone through the German-Jewish youth movement and then on to Gross-Breesen may have played its part in this judgmental display.

56. What is meant is the group at Nieuwesluis Workcamp.

57. "The Beggars," a sixteenth-century political faction opposed to Philip II and Spanish rule of the Netherlands.

58. Ernst Wiechert was a popular author of the twenties and thirties, appealing particularly to adolescents. This novel is the story of a boy of German descent raised in Malaysia by a Malaysian nanny. The boy ultimately commits suicide when he must return to East Prussia because he is homesick for Malaysia.

59. Grüssau, town in the district of Landeshut in Silesia; famous for its monastery.

60. Mr. Zimmer was an agent of the Haupttreuhandstelle Ost (HTO; Chief Property Receiver, East). This organization took over the estate from its legal owner, Willi Rohr, a Jew of Polish nationality who was then residing in Poland and had put Gross-Breesen at the disposal of the Reichsvertretung, rent-free, in 1936. Negotiations on the valuation of the property and details of the transfer that took place between the Reichsvereinigung, the successor of the Reichsvertretung, and the German governmental agencies extended over a period of five months. See Joseph Walk, ed., "The Diary of Günther Marcuse," p. 177, note 18.

61. For HTO see note 60.

62. On the last entries see Walk, ed., "The Diary of Günther Marcuse," p. 181, n. 27.

Bibliography

Adam, Uwe Dietrich. *Judenpolitik im Dritten Reich*. Düsseldorf: Droste Verlag, 1972.

Adler-Rudel, Salomon. *Jüdische Selbsthilfe unter dem Naziregime 1933–1939 im Spiegel der Berichte der Reichsvertretung der Juden in Deutschland*. Tübingen: J. C. B. Mohr (Paul Siebeck), 1974.

Allen, William S. "Die deutsche Öffentlichkeit und die 'Reichskristallnacht'—Konflikte zwischen Werthierarchie und Propaganda im Dritten Reich." In Detlev Peukert, et al, eds., *Die Reihen fest geschlossen, Beiträge zur Geschichte des Alltags unterm Nationalsozialismus*, pp. 397–411. Wuppertal: Hammer Verlag, 1981.

Angress, Werner T. "Auswandererlehrgut Gross-Breesen." *Year Book of the Leo Baeck Institute*, 10:168–87. London: East and West Library, 1965.

—— "Die 'Judenfrage' im Spiegel amtlicher Berichte 1935." In Ursula Büttner, ed. *Das Unrechtsregime. Internationale Forschung über den Nationalsozialismus*. Volume 2: *Verfolgung, Exil, belasteter Neubeginn (Festschrift für Werner Jochmann zum 65. Geburtstag)*, pp. 19–43. Hamburger Beiträge zur Sozial- und Zeitgeschichte, 22. Hamburg: Christians Verlag, 1986.

Anonymous [Günter Friedländer]. *Jüdische Jugend zwischen Gestern und Morgen*. Berlin: Vortrupp jüdischer Buchverlag, 1938.

"Arbeitsberichte der Reichsvertretung der Juden in Deutschland für das Jahr . . . [1937, 1938]" (ARV). Mimeographed. (Copies in the Archive of the Leo Baeck Institute, New York.)

"Arbeitsberichte des Zentralausschusses für Hilfe und Aufbau bei der Reichsvertretung der Juden in Deutschland, 1933–1936" (Adz). Mimeographed. (Copies in the Archive of the Leo Baeck Institute, New York.)

Baumel, Esther J. *The Rescue and Resettlement of the Jewish Refugee Children from Europe*. Ramat Gan: Bar Ilan University, 1985.

Blau, Bruno. *Das Ausnahmerecht für die Juden in Deutschland 1933–1945*.

Düsseldorf: Verlag der Allgemeinen Wochenzeitung der Juden in Deutschland, 1965.

Boas, Jacob. "The Shrinking World of German Jewry, 1933–1938." *Year Book of the Leo Baeck Institute,* 31:241–66. London: Secker and Warburg, 1986.

Borinski, Annelise Ora. *Erinnerungen, 1940–1943.* Nördlingen: Georg Wagner Verlag, 1970.

Brodnitz, Friedrich. "Jüdische Sozialarbeit in Deutschland als Einheit." *Jüdische Wohlfahrtspflege und Sozialpolitik,* n.s. (Berlin 1936), 6:90–99.

—— "Memories of the Reichsvertretung: A Personal Report." *Year Book of the Leo Baeck Institute,* 31:267–77. London: Secker and Warburg, 1986.

—— "Die Reichsvertretung der deutschen Juden." In Hans Tramer, ed., *In zwei Welten. Siegfried Moses zum 75. Geburtstag,* pp. 106–140 Tel-Aviv: Bitaon, 1962.

Broszat, Martin, et al., eds. *Bayern in der NS-Zeit.* Volume 1: *Soziale Lage und politisches Verhalten der Bevölkerung im Spiegel vertraulicher Berichte.* Munich and Vienna: Oldenbourg Verlag, 1977. Volume 2: *Herrschaft und Gesellschaft im Konflikt.* Munich and Vienna: Oldenbourg Verlag, 1979.

Buber, Martin. "Wie erziehen wir ein unbefangenes, unabhängiges neues Geschlecht?" *Bayerische Israelitische Gemeindezeitung* (August 1, 1933), vol. 9, no. 15.

Buchheim, Hans, et al., eds. *Anatomie des SS-Staates.* Volume 2: *Konzentrationslager, Kommissarbefehl, Judenverfolgung.* Olten and Freiburg: Walter Verlag, 1965.

Büttner, Ursula, ed. *Das Unrechtsregime. Internationale Forschung über den Nationalsozialismus.* Volume 2: *Verfolgung, Exil, belasteter Neubeginn (Festschrift für Werner Jochmann zum 65. Geburtstag).* Hamburger Beträge zur Sozial- und Zeitgeschichte, 22. Hamburg: Christians Verlag, 1986.

Cramer, Ernst. "Ein Amerikaner in Buchenwald: Vor sechs Jahren war ich hier KZ-ler." *Die Welt* (November 9, 1978), no. 262.

Deutschkron, Inge. *Ich trug den gelben Stern.* Cologne: Deutscher Taschenbuch Verlag, 1980.

Franck, Norbert and Gesine Asmus, eds. (Arbeitsgruppe Pädagogisches Museum). *Heil Hitler, Herr Lehrer. Volksschule 1933–1945.* Rheinbeck: Rowohlt Verlag, 1983.

Freeden, Herbert. "Bleiben oder Gehen. Die Diskussion über die Auswanderung in der jüdischen Presse in Nazideutschland." *Bulletin des Leo Baeck Instituts* (Jerusalem 1985), 70:33–54.

—— "A Jewish Theatre Under the Swastika." *Year Book of the Leo Baeck Institute,* 1:142–62. London: East and West Library, 1956.

—— *Jüdisches Theater in Nazideutschland.* Schriftenreihe wissenschaftlicher Abhandlungen des Leo Baeck Instituts, 12. Tübingen: J. C. B. Mohr (Paul Siebeck), 1964.

Freund, Julius. *O Buchenwald.* Klagenfurt: privately printed, n.d.

Giess, Horst. "Die Rolle des Reichsnährstandes im nationalsozialistischen Herrschaftssystem." In Gerhard Hirschfeld and Lothar Kettenacker, eds., *Der "Führerstaat": Mythos und Realität. Studien zur Struktur und Politik des Dritten Reiches—The "Führer-State": Myth and Reality. Studies on the Structure and Politics of the Third Reich,* pp. 270–304. Publications of the German Historical Institute, London, 8. Stuttgart: Klett-Cotta, 1981.

Genschel, Helmut. *Die Verdrängung der Juden aus der Wirtschaft im Dritten Reich.* Göttingen: Musterschmidt Verlag, 1966.

Graml, Hermann. *Der 9. November 1938. "Reichskristallnacht."* Bonn: Bundeszentrale für Heimatdienst, 1957.

Haestrup, Joergen. *Passage to Palestine: Young Jews in Denmark, 1932–1945.* Odense: Odense University Press, 1983.

Hannam, Charles. *A Boy in That Situation: An Autobiography.* New York: Harper and Row, 1986.

Herrmann, Gert-Julius. "Jüdische Jugend in der Verfolgung. Eine Studie über das Schicksal jüdischer Jugendlicher aus Württemberg und Hohenzollern." Ph.D. diss., University of Tübingen, 1967.

Hilberg, Raul. *The Destruction of the European Jews.* Chicago: Quadrangle Books, 1961.

Hoffmann, Bruno. "Die Ausnahmegesetzgebung gegen die Juden von 1933–1945 unter besonderer Berücksichtigung der Synagogengemeinde Köln." Ph.D. diss., University of Cologne, n.d.

Homeyer, Friedel. *Beitrag zur Geschichte der Gartenbauschule Ahlem 1893–1979.* Hanover: Landkreis und Landwirtschaftskammer, 1980.

Internationales Buchenwald-Komitee et al., *Buchenwald. Mahnung und Verpflichtung. Dokumente und Berichte.* East Berlin: Kongress Verlag, n.d. (1959).

Internationales Militärtribunal (IMT). *Der Prozess gegen die Hauptkriegsverbrecher vor dem Internationalen Militärgerichtshof.* 42 vols. Nuremberg: Militärgerichtshof, 1947–49.

Josephthal, Georg. "Die Berufsfrage der jüdischen Jugend." *Gemeinschaftsarbeit der jüdische Jugend* . . . (Berlin 1937), pp. 40–48.

—— "Pädagogische und auswanderungspolitische Gesichtspunkte des jüdischen Berufsbildungswerks in Deutschland." *Jüdische Wohlfahrtspflege und Sozialpolitik* (Berlin 1938), 8:6.

Kershaw, Ian. *Popular Opinion and Political Dissent in the Third Reich: Bavaria, 1933–1945.* Oxford: Oxford University Press, 1983.

Kimche, Jon and D. Kimche. *The Secret Roads: The "Illegal" Migration of a People, 1938–1948.* London, 1954.

Kindt, Werner, ed. *Die deutsche Jugendbewegung 1920–1933. Die bündische Zeit. Quellenschriften.* Cologne: Diederichs Verlag, 1974.

Kochan, Lionel. *Pogrom: November 10, 1938*. London: A. Deutsch Press, 1957.

König, Joel [pseud. Esra Feinberg]. *David. Aufzeichnungen eines Überlebenden*. Frankfurt am Main: Fischer Taschenbuch Verlag, 1979.

Kogon, Eugen. *Der SS-Staat. Das System der deutschen Konzentrationslager*. Frankfurt am Main: Europäische Verlagsanstalt, 1961.

—— *The Theory and Practice of Hell: The German Concentration Camps and the System Behind Them*. New York: Farrar, Straus, and Cudahy, 1950.

Konzentrationslager Buchenwald. Bericht des Internationalen Lagerkomitees. Weimar: Thüringer Volksverlag, 1949.

Kranzler, David H. *Japanese, Nazis, and Jews: The Jewish Refugee Community of Shanghai, 1938–1945*. New York: Yeshiva University Press, 1976.

Kwiet, Konrad and Helmut Eschwege, eds. *Selbstbehauptung und Widerstand. Deutsche Juden im Kampf um Existenz und Menschenwürde 1933–1945*. Hamburg: Christians Verlag, 1984.

Landenberger, Hilde. "Die soziale Funktion der jüdischen Jugendbewegung." *Jüdische Wohlfahrtspflege und Sozialpolitik* (Berlin 1936), 6:99–106.

Laqueur, Walter Z. *Young Germany: A History of the German Youth Movement*. London: Routledge and Kegan Paul, 1962.

Lemle, Heinrich. *Jüdische Jugend in Aufbruch. Ein Wort an Alle*. Frankfurt am Main: J. Kauffman Verlag, 1935.

Leshem, Perez. *Strasse zur Rettung 1933–1939. Aus Deutschland vertrieben, bereitet sich die jüdische Jugend auf Palästina vor*. Tel Aviv: Verband der Freunde der Histadrut, 1973.

Lexikon des Judentums. Ed. Emanuel Bin Gorion, Ernst G. Lowenthal, and Hans G. Reissner. Gütersloh: Bertelsmann Verlag, 1967.

Lowenthal, Ernst G. "The Ahlem Experiment: A Brief Survey of the 'Jüdische Gartenbauschule.'" *Year Book of the Leo Baeck Institute*, 14:165–81. London: East and West Library, 1969.

—— *Bewährung im Untergang. Ein Gedenkbuch*. Stuttgart: Deutsche Verlagsanstalt, 1966.

—— *Juden in Preussen. Biographisches Verzeichnis. Ein repräsentativer Querschnitt*. Berlin: Bildarchiv Preussischer Kulturbesitz, 1981.

Manowitz, Rosalyn, ed. *Reflections on the Holocaust: In Commemoration of the Fortieth Anniversary of "Kristallnacht" November 9–10, 1938—November 10, 1978*. New York: Hebrew Tabernacle Congregation of Washington Heights, New York City, 1978.

Meier-Cronemeyer, Hermann. "Jüdische Jugendbewegung." *Germania Judaica* (Cologne 1969), 8:1–122. Kölner Bibliothek zur Geschichte des Deutschen Judentums.

Melitz, Rudolf, ed. *Das ist unser Weg. Junge Juden schildern Umschichtung und Hachscharah*. Berlin: Joachim Goldstein Verlag, 1937.

Mommsen, Hans. "Der nationalsozialistische Polizeistaat und die Juden-verfolgung vor 1938. Dokumentation." *Vierteljahrshefte für Zeitgeschichte* (1962), 10:68–87.

Mosse, George L. *Germans and Jews: The Right, the Left, and the Search for a "Third Force" in Pre-Nazi Germany.* New York: Howard Fertig, 1970.

Paucker, Arnold, ed. *Die Juden im nationalsozialistischen Deutschland—The Jews in Nazi Germany, 1933–1943.* Schriftenreihe wissenschaftlicher Abhandlungen des Leo Baeck Instituts, 45. Tübingen: J. C. B. Mohr (Paul Siebeck), 1986.

—— and Lucien Steinberg. "Some Notes on Resistance." *Year Book of the Leo Baeck Institute,* 16:239–48. London: East and West Library, 1971.

Paxton, Robert O. and Michael R. Marrus. *Vichy France and the Jews.* New York: Basic Books, 1981.

Pikarski, Margot. *Jugend im Berliner Widerstand. Herbert Baum und Kampfgefährten.* East Berlin: Militärverlag der Deutschen Demokratischen Republik, 1971.

Pingel, Falk. *Häftlinge unter SS—Herrschaft. Widerstand, Selbstbehauptung und Vernichtung im Konzentrationslager.* Hamburg: Hoffmann und Campe Verlag, 1978.

Platner, Geert et al., eds. *Schule im Dritten Reich. Erziehung zum Tod? Eine Dokumentation.* Munich: Deutscher Taschenbuch Verlag, 1983.

Poller, Walter. *Arztschreiber in Buchenwald. Bericht des Häftlings 996 aus Block 36.* Hanover: Phönix Verlag, 1960.

Rehme, Günter and Konstantin Haase. . . . *mit Rumpf und Stumpf ausrotten. Zur Geschichte der Juden in Marburg und Umgebung nach 1933.* Marburg: Presseamt der Stadt Marburg, 1982.

Reichsausschuss der jüdischen Jugendverbände, ed. *Gemeinschaftsarbeit der jüdischen Jugend. Aus der Arbeit des Reichsausschusses der jüdischen Jugendverbände 1922–1936.* Berlin: Zentralwohlfahrtsstelle der Juden in Deutschland, 1937.

Reinharz, Jehuda. "Hashomer Hazair in Nazi Germany." In Arnold Paucker, ed., *Die Juden im nationalsozialistischen Deutschland—The Jews in Nazi Germany, 1933–1943,* pp. 317–50. Schriftenreihe wissenschaftlicher Abhandlungen des Leo Baeck Instituts, 45. Tübingen: J. C. B. Mohr (Paul Siebeck), 1986.

Rheins, Carl J. "German Jewish Patriotism, 1918–1935: A Study of the Attitudes and Actions of the Reichsbund jüdischer Frontsoldaten, the Verband nationaldeutscher Juden, the Schwarzes Fähnlein, Jungenschaft, and the Deutscher Vortrupp, Gefolgschaft deutscher Juden." Ph.D. diss., State University of New York at Stony Brook, 1978.

—— "The Schwarzes Fähnlein, Jungenschaft, 1932–1934." *Year Book of the Leo Baeck Institute,* 23:173–97. London: Secker and Warburg, 1978.

Richarz, Monika, ed. *Jüdisches Leben in Deutschland.* Volume 3: *Selbst-*

zeugnisse zur Sozialgeschichte 1918–1945. Stuttgart: Deutsche Verlagsanstalt, 1982.

Rinott, Chanoch. "Major Trends in Jewish Youth Movements in Germany." *Year Book of the Leo Baeck Institute,* 19:77–95. London: Secker and Warburg, 1974.

Rosenheim, Käthe. "Jüdische Sozialarbeit in Deutschland als Einheit. 1. Internationale Kinderfürsorge." *Jüdische Wohlfahrtspflege und Sozialpolitik* (Berlin 1936), 6:93–97.

Rosenstock, Werner. "The Jewish Youth Movement." *Year Book of the Leo Baeck Institute,* 19:97–105. London: Secker and Warburg, 1974.

Rosenthal, Hans. *Zwei Leben in Deutschland.* Bergisch-Gladbach: Lübbe Verlag, 1980.

Schatzker, Chaim. "Martin Buber's Influence on the Jewish Youth Movement in Germany." *Year Book of the Leo Baeck Institute,* 23:151–71. London: Secker and Warburg, 1978.

Schleunes, Karl A. *The Twisted Road to Auschwitz: Nazi Policy Toward German Jews, 1933–1939.* Urbana: University of Illinois Press, 1970.

Scholl, Inge. *The White Rose: Munich, 1942–1943.* Middletown, Conn.: Wesleyan University Press, 1983.

Scholtz, Harald. *Erziehung und Unterricht unterm Hakenkreuz.* Göttingen: Vandenhoeck and Ruprecht Verlag, 1985.

Semprun, Jorge. *Was für ein schöner Sonntag!* Frankfurt am Main: Suhrkamp Verlag, 1981.

Senger, Valentin. *Kaiserhofstrasse 12.* Darmstadt and Neuwied: Luchterhand Verlag, 1980.

Stegeman, H. B. J. and J. P. Vorsteveld. *Het Joodse Werkdorp in de Wieringermeer, 1934–1941.* Zutphen: Walburg Pers, 1983.

Stern, Eva Michaelis. "Erinnerungen an die Anfänge der Jugendalijah in Deutschland." *Bulletin des Leo Baeck Instituts* (Jerusalem 1985), 70:55–66.

Stern, Heinemann. *Warum hassen sie uns eigentlich? Jüdisches Leben zwischen den Kriegen. Erinnerungen.* Commentary by Hans Ch. Meyer. Düsseldorf: Droste Verlag, 1970.

Strauss, Herbert A. "Jewish Emigration from Germany. 1. Nazi Policies and Jewish Responses." *Year Book of the Leo Baeck Institute,* 25:313–63. London: Secker and Warburg, 1980.

Tijn, Gertrude van. "Werkdorp Nieuwesluis." *Year Book of the Leo Baeck Institute,* 14:182–99. London: East and West Library, 1969.

Tokayer, Marvin. *The Fugu Plan: On the Untold Story of the Japanese and the Jews During World War II.* New York: Paddington Press, 1979.

Vinke, Hermann. *The Short Life of Sophie Scholl.* New York: Harper and Row, 1984.

Walk, Joseph. "The Diary of Günter Marcuse (The Last Days of the Gross-Breesen Training Centre)." *Yad Vashem Studies on the European Jewish Catastrophe and Resistance* (Jerusalem 1970), 8:159–81.

—— "Jüdische Schüler an deutschen Schulen in Nazideutschland." *Bulletin des Leo Baeck Instituts* (Jerusalem, 1980), 19:101–9.
—— *Das Sonderrecht für die Juden im NS-Staat. Eine Sammlung der gesetzlichen Massnahmen und Richtlinien.* Heidelberg and Karlsruhe: C. F. Müller Verlag, 1981.
Winterfeld, Hans. "Deutschland: Ein Zeitbild 1926–1945. Leidensweg eines deutschen Juden in den ersten 19 Jahren seines Lebens." Manuscript, n.d. Archive of the Leo Baeck Institute, New York.
Zahnwetzer, Moritz. *KZ Buchenwald. Erlebnisbericht.* Kasssel: privately printed, n.d.

Index

Adler, Karl (musicologist), 56
Adler-Rudel, Salomon, 36
Ahlem (training center), 22, 39, 42
Ahrensdorf (training center), 38
Aid Society of the Jews in Germany, 59
Aktion, see Crystal Night
Aktionsjuden, see Crystal Night
Aliyah, 26, 27, 29, 38, 159n; *see also* Emigration
American Jewish Joint Distribution Committee, 60
Anti-Jewish measures, 1-3, 8-12, 16, 19, 23, 32, 33-34, 38-39, 61-63, 155-56nn; yellow star mandatory, 39-40, 161n; *see also* Anti-Semitism; Crystal Night
Anti-Semitism, 4, 6-12 passim, 16-17, 23-25, 33, 63; *see also* Anti-Jewish measures; Crystal Night
Argentina project, 60, 75, 110, 119, 127, 164n
Assimilation, *see* Jews, assimilated
"Atonement" payment, 35
Augstein, Rudolf, 11
Auschwitz (concentration camp), 3, 42, 72, 73, 74, 78
Australia project, 71, 75, 108, 114, 119, 121, 134, 140-44, 170n

Bachad, *see* Brith Chaluzim Datiim
Baeck, Leo, Rabbi Dr., 44
Baum, Herbert, 41, 162n
Berger, Rifka (trainee), 42
Bernstein, Walter, 72, 73, 122

Black Troop, Boys' Force, 19, 51
Blue-White, *Bund* for Young Jewish Hikers in Germany (Blau-Weiss, Bund für jüdisches Jugendwandern in Deutschland), 18
Bondy, Curt: arrest and imprisonment, 61, 67-68, 70; correspondence with F. W. Borchardt, 126-27; correspondence with Haka, 120-21; correspondence with O. Hirsch, 116-17; correspondence with F. Schwarzschild, 121-22; correspondence with J. L. Seligsohn, 136-37; correspondence with Töpper [and Meui], 106-7, 118-20, 133, 137-38; correspondence with G. van Tijn, 107-9; correspondence with D. Warmbrunn, 103; and educational methods, 47-49; emigration of, 71; personal background, 44-45, 57
Bondy, Fritz, 87, 89, 90, 94, 96, 99, 168n
Borchardt, Frederick [Fritz] W., 88, 91, 106, 168n
Bosi (trainee), 143
Boycott Day *1933*, 2
Braun, Mösch (trainee), 114
Brazil project, *see* Paraná [Brazil] project
"Briefe an die alten Gross-Breesener," *see* Circular letter, Gross-Breesen
Brith Chaluzim Datiim (Bachad), 26, 27, 28
Brötchen (trainee), 125, 126

184 INDEX

Jewish population statistics, 7-8, 157n
Jewish School of Horticulture at Ahlem, see Ahlem (training center)
Jewish schools, 8-17, 20, 35, 41; see also Occupational training centers
Jewish War Veterans League, 22, 51, 162-63nn
Jewish Workcamp Nieuwesluis, 71, 72, 78, 87, 89, 90, 92, 93, 94, 95, 99, 105, 107, 108, 109, 112, 114, 115, 125, 126, 131, 135-36, 141, 168n, 171n
Jews, assimilated, 4-6, 25-26, 57; see also Jewish identity; Judaism
Jochen, see Feingold, Jochen
Johnny (trainee), 143
Jonny, see Hackmann, Hermann
Joodse Werkdorp Niewesluis, see Jewish Workcamp Nieuwesluis
Josephthal, Georg, 27, 157n
Judaism, 4-5, 20-21, 26, 57-58; self-defined, 36
Judengesetzgebung, see Anti-Jewish measures
Jüdisches Hilfswerk, 45
Jüdische Landarbeit GmbH, 22
Jüdische Rundschau, 43
Jugendverband der Staatszionisten, 24
Juwa, 86, 94, 101, 105, 113

Karlsberg, Bernhard, Dr., 127, 128, 171n
Karminski, Hannah, 117, 170n
Kaufmann, Hugo, 126
Kellerman, Heinz, 85, 88, 95, 96, 163n, 168n
Kenya project, 60, 71, 75, 92, 102, 108, 110, 114, 119
Kitchener Camp, 71, 122, 126, 130, 132, 171n
Kiwi, Hermann (training assistant), 46, 94, 105, 124-25
Kiwi, Max, 46, 55, 62, 64, 67, 72
Klaus (trainee), 143
Klobü (trainee), 86
Knirps (trainee), 86, 94
"Knowing Life" seminars, see Lebenskunde

Koch, Karl (SS colonel), 65
König, Joel, 7, 13, 30-31, 40, 42
Krause (teamster), 62
Kristallnacht, see Crystal Night
Kulturbund deutscher Juden, see Cultural Association of German Jews

Landesbauernschaft, 63
Land Settlement Association of Silesia (Landsiedlungsgesellschaft), 150, 152
Law Against Overcrowding of German Schools and Universities, 8
League of Jewish War Veterans, see Jewish War Veterans League
League of Jewish Youth, see Ring, League of German Jewish Youth
Lebenskunde, 48, 68, 138
Lehmann, Ilse, Dr., 71
Leo (trainee), 143
Leschnitzer, Adolf, 14-16, 157-58nn
Leus (trainee), 86, 87, 94, 98
Lichtenstein, Heinz, 114
Loewensberg, Ernst, 78, 93
Loewensberg, Joseph, 78, 87, 93, 123; correspondence with Töpper, 88, 94-96, 100-1
Löwenstein, Leo, Dr., 163n

Makkabi Hazair, 27
Manfred (trainee), 86
Marcuse, Günther (trainee), 78-80; diary entries, 144-54
Mauthausen (concentration camp), 72, 170n
Mayer, Paul Yogi, 51
Mende (farm manager), 152, 154
Menschenkunde, see Lebenskunde
Meui (friend of trainees), 77, 78, 83, 87, 89, 90, 93, 97, 98, 99, 101, 106, 133
Meyer, Traute, 46
Meyrowitz, Hilde, 88, 168n
Müller, Heinrich (Gestapo official), 39, 64
Muller, Irmgard (trainee), 160n